A taste of
BIRMINGHAM
Volume·II

A taste of
BIRMINGHAM
Volume II

First published 2004
by Midland Independent Magazines
Weaman Street, Birmingham B4 6AT

ISBN 0-9543388-4-7

Editor: Stacey Barnfield
Copy Editors: Louise Palfreyman and Jon Perks
Product Manager: Anthony Bisseker
Photography: Craig Holmes and Edward Moss
Production Manager: Julia Gregory
Thanks to Bill Green Photography, Kenilworth

Printed by Butler & Tanner Group, Frome, Somerset.

A Trinity Mirror business

A taste of
BIRMINGHAM
Volume·II

PHOTOGRAPHY BY CRAIG HOLMES
AND EDWARD MOSS

CONTENTS

ALL DISHES ARE BASED ON A SERVING OF FOUR, UNLESS OTHERWISE STATED.

FOREWORD

"Who said there was nothing outside London when it comes to good food?"

Having joined the Birmingham marketplace back in December 2003 with my latest Restaurant Paris, located within The Mailbox, I have been overwhelmed with the tremendous support and welcome I have received from the public and my fellow colleagues in the catering and hospitality industry.

Birmingham has seen dramatic changes over the past ten years with new apartments springing up at every turn, this revolution of city living and increasing population has resulted in creating a bigger demand for entertaining and dining. The explosion of fantastic eateries spread in and around the region offer a choice and quality rivalling all other UK cities.

The dining out culture has surpassed all expectations; I alone have never seen a city drink as much Champagne – not just house Champagne but Grand Marques such as Krug, Dom Perignon, Roederer and Bollinger and in varying vintages!

The people of Birmingham have discerning palates, knowledge of food and make high demands; fortunately there are operators in the city who can deliver.

This book brings together a collection of chefs, cooks and restaurateurs and gives a small snapshot of the different styles and origins of cooking; their passion is evident through this collection of recipes and photographs, expressing the best of what they have to offer.

I would like you to read this book and be inspired, be adventurous and possibly try out some of the dishes or simply use it as a guide as to what Birmingham has on offer.

"The essence of good food is simplicity."

Patrick McDonald

Make your reservation...

A taste of
BIRMINGHAM
Volume·II

BAR ESTILO

Chris Childs,
general manager

BAR ESTILO

The first Bar Estilo to open outside Greater London was voted Best Restaurant 2003 in the Birmingham Nightlife Awards. It is a buzzing eatery serving Mediterranean and tapas cuisine with a twist.

There are around 30 tapas-style starters to choose from, evenly divided between meat, seafood and vegetarian, and 16 mains ranging from paellas, chicken, fish and steak dishes, ensuring that all palates are catered for.

'Estilo' means style in Spanish, and the decor and ambience at Bar Estilo Birmingham lives up to the name. The bar area is stunning, with comfy sofas that add to the relaxed vibe – Bar Estilo is a great place to chill out before or after dinner. A great range of cocktails, wines and speciality beers are available, so whether you just fancy a quick drink at the end of a hard afternoon's shopping, a jug of sangria and tapas with a few friends or a three-course dinner that won't break the bank you will not be disappointed.

Noted for "the friendliest waiting staff around," Bar Estilo is ideally situated in the prestigious Mailbox development just five minutes walk from New Street station. Doors open daily from noon until 11pm (10.30pm Sun) and there is seating for 150 inside, plus a great terrace overlooking the canal for al fresco dining – a great spot to watch the world go by on a sunny day!

David Charalambous
Managing director

Chorizo and feta cheese tortilla

Serves 4-6

INGREDIENTS

6 eggs
100ml milk
250g potatoes
150g cooking chorizo
200g feta cheese
Fresh ground pepper
Olive oil

METHOD

Peel the potatoes and cut into 1.5cm slices.

Fry the chorizo in a little oil in a non-stick pan until cooked through. Remove from the pan (retain the juice to cook the potatoes – this will give the tortilla a vibrant colour). Cool the chorizo slightly then slice.

Add the slices of potato to the pan with the chorizo juice and cook the potatoes slowly until soft (add a little olive oil if necessary).

Beat the eggs in a bowl with the milk, add the cooked potatoes, sliced chorizo and crumble in the feta cheese.

Mix all the ingredients together and season with fresh ground pepper. (Feta cheese is quite salty so you shouldn't need additional salt).

Return ingredients to the frying pan and cook over a low heat for three to four minutes. When the tortilla is firm, place a plate over the top of the pan and turn the tortilla out onto the plate, carefully slide the tortilla back into the pan and cook for a further two to three minutes to brown the other side.

Turn out onto a serving plate, leave for about five minutes, cut into slices and serve.

To serve
Either cut into small squares and serve with cocktail sticks as a tapas or garnish with some simply dressed leaves as a starter or light lunch.

BAR ESTILO
110 -114 Wharfside Street, The Mailbox, Birmingham B1 1RF
Tel: 0121 643 3443
www.barestilo.co.uk

Salmon fillet with mango salsa and sweet potato mash

Serves 6

6 salmon fillets
Salt and pepper to season

Coriander butter
15g coriander
125g unsalted butter

Sweet potato mash
1kg sweet potatoes
1kg mashing potatoes (eg Maris piper)
50g butter
Salt and pepper

Mango salsa
2 large ripe mangoes
4 spring onions
$^1/_2$ red onion
2 tomatoes
1 red chilli
15g coriander
1tsp salt
1tsp pepper
50ml fresh orange juice
50ml olive oil

Coriander butter
Soften the butter (do not melt). Finely chop the coriander. Mix together and refrigerate until needed.

Salmon
Season the salmon with salt and pepper. Oil grill pan and heat until smoking hot or preheat grill. Cook the salmon on both sides until brown. Place on an ovenproof tray with a 25-30g of coriander butter on each fillet. Place in the oven at 180°C for five minutes or until the butter is melted and the salmon is cooked through.

Mango salsa
Peel the mangoes and cut into 1cm cubes. Finely slice the spring onion. Finely chop the red onion and chilli. Deseed the tomatoes and cut into small dice. Finely chop the coriander. Mix all of these with remaining salsa ingredients. Refrigerate until required.

Sweet potato mash
Peel the sweet potatoes and the potatoes. Cut into large pieces.
   Place in separate saucepans of cold salted water. Bring both to the boil and simmer until the potatoes are cooked. Drain and then mix the two in a large pot. Add the butter and mash together until smooth. Season with salt and pepper to taste. Keep warm whilst preparing the salmon.

To serve
Place the mash and the salsa side by side in the centre of the plate. Sit the salmon carefully against the mash. Drizzle the butter over the salmon and garnish with wedges of fresh lime.

BAR ESTILO
110 -114 Wharfside Street, The Mailbox, Birmingham B1 1RF
Tel: 0121 643 3443
www.barestilo.co.uk

Lemon crema Catalan

INGREDIENTS

6 eggs	200g caster sugar
300ml whipping cream	4 lemons
200ml milk	Redcurrants and sprig of mint to serve

METHOD

Grate the zest of the lemons and squeeze the juice. Whisk the eggs and sugar in a bowl and stir in the lemon zest and juice. Lightly whisk in the cream and milk.

Divide the mixture into six terracotta dishes or ramekins.

Place in a baking tray and fill up to half the level of the dishes with hot water, taking care not to get water into the desserts.

Bake in the oven at 160°C for about 20 minutes or until just set.

Allow to cool then sprinkle the top of each one with sugar. Place the Catalans under a very hot grill until the sugar caramelises.

To serve

Garnish with a little fresh fruit such as redcurrants and a sprig of fresh mint to give colour.

BAR ESTILO
110 -114 Wharfside Street, The Mailbox, Birmingham B1 1RF
Tel: 0121 643 3443
www.barestilo.co.uk

CAFÉ IKON

*Head chef
Roy Bogle*

CAFÉ IKON

In 2004 Ikon gallery celebrated 40 years since its inception in a small kiosk in the old Bull Ring at the top of Digbeth High Street.

We at Café Ikon had the privilege of hosting a lunch to celebrate an exhibition of work by some of the artists who founded Ikon, some of whom had not seen each other for a very long time. In conversation with these founding fathers and mothers it was obvious their passion for art and design had not diminished and their sense of pride and ownership of what had been conceived in a gallery without walls was obvious.

I am proud to say that that sense of ownership spills into the café – which celebrated its sixth birthday in 2004 – by visitors and customers who continue to support us and bring back their friends, family and, I'm happy to say, new families time and again.

Over the past few years we have seen the birth of new Ikon babies who we hope to welcome as friends and customers in the next 40 years.

James Marsden
Chef/patron

Tortilla Espanola

INGREDIENTS

1kg thinly sliced peeled potatoes

1 large Spanish onion (diced)

300ml good olive oil

9 eggs (beaten)

Seasoning

METHOD

Simmer the potatoes and onion in the olive oil for about 20 minutes taking care not to burn.

All the mix to cool a little and strain the solids from the oil (retain for future use). Add the warm mix to the egg and seasoning (if the mix is too warm the eggs will scramble). Tip into a hot, oiled frying pan. Shake the pan to ensure the omelette does not stick and slide a wooden spoon around the edge to form a neat wall around the tortilla.

After about ten minutes or when the mix is fairly firm, flip the omelette onto a large plate or tray and return to the hot frying pan to cook the underside for a further ten minutes.

Turn out onto a fresh plate and serve hot or cold with salad, ham or between bread as the king of Spanish sandwiches – Bocadilla de Tortilla.

Special note

After the potato and onion has been cooked any number of other ingredients could be added: fried peppers or courgettes; spinach and cheese; tuna; chorizo or ham.

CAFÉ IKON
Ikon Gallery, 1 Oozells Square, Brindleyplace, Birmingham B1 2HS
Tel: 0121 248 3226

Chuletas de cordero
(lamb cutlet)

INGREDIENTS

1kg best end lamb cutlets	1 red pepper (diced)
Seasoning	1 small red onion (diced)
Cream sherry	20g pine nuts
	100g fried bread (crushed)
400g morcilla – Spanish black pudding	1tbsp quince paste or fruit conserve
1 carrot (diced)	60ml meat or vegetable stock

METHOD

Into a hot oiled pan seal the seasoned cutlets for one minute either side. Flambe with 1tbsp of cream sherry and remove to a hot grill.

In the hot pan fry the onions, carrots and pepper until soft. Remove the morcilla from its skin and add to the vegetables, stirring so they are well mixed. Add the pine nuts and crushed fried bread and form into a patty in the centre of a warm plate.

Reduce half a glass of red wine and the same amount of meat or vegetable stock with the quince paste (membrillo) or other preferred fruit conserve to a thick sauce consistency and drizzle over the lamb and morcilla mix.

To serve
Accompany with fried broad beans, with pancetta or jamon serrano. Alternatively use the mix to stuff a boned saddle of lamb.

CAFÉ IKON
Ikon Gallery, 1 Oozells Square, Brindleyplace, Birmingham B1 2HS
Tel: 0121 248 3226

Bunuelos de manzana
(pancakes with apple and cream)

INGREDIENTS

150g plain flour

50g caster sugar

75ml soured cream

Pinch salt

3 eggs

5g bicarb of soda

25g cream of tartar (leavening agent)

100ml cold water

150ml milk

4 cooking apples

50ml water or liquor

100-150g demerara sugar

Pinch of cinnamon to taste

Icing sugar to dredge

Fruits to decorate

METHOD

Beat together the flour, sugar, soured cream, salt and eggs. Mix together the bicarb, tartar and water and add to the batter. Gradually add the milk to the mixture to a wet consistency.

Pour into a hot buttered pan and allow the mixture to spread to a thin, lacey consistency – add more milk if too thick.

In a heavy saucepan place the peeled apples, sugar and cinnamon (add unsalted butter if you want a luxurious apple, almost toffee taste). Add 50ml of water (or brandy, calvados or liquor of choice) and slowly reduce the apples to a mushy texture (I like to keep it quite chunky). Remove from the heat and allow to cool a little. Place the filling in one corner of the crepe and quarter the pancake around, dredge with icing sugar and place under a hot grill to caramelise.

Serve with either fresh whipped cream, crème fraiche or ice cream and preserved fruits.

CAFÉ IKON
Ikon Gallery, 1 Oozells Square, Brindleyplace, Birmingham B1 2HS
Tel: 0121 248 3226

CITY CAFÉ

CITY CAFÉ

City Café, in the heart of Brindleyplace, provides a stylish backdrop where four contemporary European menus are served each day created using the finest quality local ingredients.

In addition to the à la carte menu, there is an impressive Garden menu, proving that vegetarian food can be both innovative and exciting. The daily-changing kitchen menu showcases the talents of the kitchen brigade.

Finally the terrace menu serves lighter dishes that can be enjoyed al fresco style on either of the two terraces – weather permitting. In addition to the wonderful dishes on offer, City Café boasts an affordable and comprehensive wine list, featuring New and Old World wines.

Over the last 15 years the head chef, Colin Layfield, has established an impeccable record working with talented chefs, including Bruno Loubet and Anthony Demetri in restaurants such as Harvey Nichols-owned Prism, 3AA rosette L'Odéon and the two-Michelin-starred Four Seasons.

Lobster bisque and skewered sea bass

INGREDIENTS

4oz butter	100ml Pernod
Shell from one large lobster, crushed	100ml brandy
2 banana shallots, chopped	100ml Noilly Prat
2 carrots, chopped	200ml white wine
5 sticks celery, chopped	2tbsp tomato purée
$\frac{1}{2}$ bulb fennel, chopped	$\frac{1}{4}$ bunch thyme
2 cloves garlic, crushed	2 bay leaves
20g dried coriander	4 pints chicken stock
20g dried fennel	2oz butter
1 star anise	1tbsp crème fraiche
3 cardamom pods	1 fillet sea bass, cubed, put onto 4
1g saffron	skewers

METHOD

Melt the butter in a heavy pan, and cook shell, shallots, carrots, celery, fennel and crushed garlic for ten minutes until vegetables are soft.

Stir in star anise, cardamom and saffron and cook for a further five minutes, pour in all the alcohol and reduce by two-thirds.

Stir in tomato purée, thyme and bay leaves, cover with chicken stock – bring to the boil and simmer for 30-40 minutes.

Strain through a fine wire sieve.

Reduce liquid by two-thirds, whisk in the second amount of butter and crème fraiche.

Season and serve with seabass skewers which have been chargrilled for four minutes, turning after two minutes.

CITY CAFÉ

City Inn Birmingham, 1 Brunswick Square, Brindleyplace, Birmingham B1 2HW
Tel: 0121 633 6300
www.citycafe.co.uk

Assiette of veal osso bucco

A stew made from muscle of veal and knuckle bone

INGREDIENTS

Osso bucco

1tbsp oil
2 large veal shins
2 carrots, chopped
2 banana shallots, chopped
3 sticks celery, chopped
2 cloves garlic
200ml white wine
1tbsp tomato purée
1 bunch thyme
2 pints chicken stock

Accompaniment

2 jacket potatoes, scrubbed
500g butter
150ml chicken stock
6 carrots (for carrot purée)
20g butter
200g veal sweetbread
4oz clarified butter
2tsp finely chopped rosemary
1 bunch pak choi
2oz butter
6oz veal fillets, cut into 4 medallions

METHOD

Heat oil in a heavy-based pan, brown the veal shin, vegetables and garlic for ten minutes. Pour in wine and reduce by two-thirds. Stir in tomato purée and thyme, cover with chicken stock and bring to the boil and simmer for three to four hours until tender. Remove meat, pass sauce through chinois.

Reduce sauce until thick enough to coat meat, return meat to pan and keep warm until ready to serve.

For the fondant potato, cut jacket potatoes into small wedges and season.

Melt butter in heavy based pan. Toss potatoes into butter, cover with chicken stock, cook slowly for 30-40 minutes, turning once.

Carrot purée

Cook carrots in boiling water until tender, purée them in a blender with butter, and season to taste. Keep warm until ready to serve.

Sweetbreads

Cover with boiling water for five minutes then refresh in iced water. Remove sinew and veins, sauté in clarified butter for four minutes, season well, add chopped rosemary before serving.

For the fillet, chargrill for two minutes on each side and serve immediately.

For the pak choi, cut the white stem into two-inch batons, heat butter and toss until wilted, season and serve immediately.

Assemble ingredients on the plates, and serve with the osso bucco.

CITY CAFÉ

City Inn Birmingham, 1 Brunswick Square, Brindleyplace, Birmingham B1 2HW
Tel: 0121 633 6300
www.citycafe.co.uk

Banana and caramel mousse

INGREDIENTS

Cases

100g plain chocolate

Mousse

250g sugar

500ml water

6 egg yolks

One leaf of gelatine, soaked in cold water until soft (approx 2 mins)

600ml whipped cream

Butterscotch sauce

100g butter

100g sugar

100ml double cream

$^1/_2$ banana, sliced

1 shot of rum (50cl)

METHOD

Melt the chocolate and spread a 6" circle over acetate paper or cling film.

Mould into metal rings and leave to set, then remove acetate.

To make the mousse, put sugar in a heavy-based pan and dissolve over low heat.

Cook until it becomes dark caramel, then carefully add the water. Cook until the mixture forms a soft ball when dropped into cold water.

Whisk the egg yolks until pale and fluffy. Add soaked gelatine, whisk until cool, fold in the whipped cream, pour into the chocolate cases.

To make the sauce, melt the butter in a heavy-based pan, dissolve sugar into it, stirring constantly. Cook until caramel is formed. Stir in cream, banana and rum, serve warm, spooned around the caramel mousse.

CITY CAFÉ

City Inn Birmingham, 1 Brunswick Square, Brindleyplace, Birmingham B1 2HW
Tel: 0121 633 6300
www.citycafe.co.uk

CORNERFLAG RESTAURANT

CORNERFLAG RESTAURANT

More than just 90 minutes!

Our new-look Cornerflag Restaurant, with unique views of the Villa Park pitch, now offers contemporary and stylish dining throughout the week – not just on match days. And, with a menu combining traditional British classics and modern cuisine, Peter Reed and our in-house brigade of chefs offer something for everyone. Our appealing and well thought-out menu is changed fortnightly with daily specials.

At the Cornerflag Restaurant we are committed to top quality food presented simply and stylishly, with an emphasis on excellent customer service. We only source the finest fresh ingredients and wherever possible use local suppliers.

Easy to find, with ample secure car parking, the Cornerflag Restaurant offers a relaxed dining experience, while the décor reflects Aston Villa Football Club's proud footballing heritage.

The Cornerflag Restaurant is open for lunches Sunday to Friday from 12-3pm, and Saturday evenings for dinner from 7.30pm. We can also offer the restaurant for private hire for that special occasion or corporate use, and we are licensed for wedding ceremonies.

You can even take your visit into extra-time by arranging a tour of Villa Park.

The Cornerflag Restaurant – it really is dining with a unique outlook!

Meli-melo of smoked and wild salmon with dill crème fraiche

INGREDIENTS

300g fresh wild salmon fillet (in season) or best quality Scottish salmon fillet skinned and pin boned

300g thinly sliced smoked salmon

100g clarified butter – butter made clear by gentle heating and impurities removed

2 fresh limes segmented, reserving any juice

200g crème fraiche

2 sprigs of fresh dill

20g Sevruga caviar

Fresh mill pepper

Salt

METHOD

Slice the fresh salmon very thinly lengthways down the fillet toward the tail. Any fine fishmonger will be able to do this.

Melt the clarified butter ready for compiling the dish.

Brush four starter size service dishes very lightly with the clarified butter and season with a twist of fresh mill pepper.

Arrange the sliced smoked salmon over the plate leaving a space around the edge of the plate so the fresh salmon slightly overlaps.

With some of the reserved lime juice drizzle a little over the smoked salmon.

Arrange the sliced wild salmon over the smoked salmon and then lightly brush with more clarified butter.

Season with salt and pepper mill.

This dish can be prepared well in advance and kept in the refrigerator until ready for cooking.

Dill crème fraiche

Chop half of the dill and mix with the crème fraiche and add a little lime juice and season.

With any leftover clarified butter, keep liquid and add the Sevruga caviar.

To cook preheat oven to 170°C. Place salmon plates into oven and gently cook for four minutes or until the salmon is just cooked without colour.

To serve spoon over each dish evenly with the caviar butter, arrange four lime segments on each dish and finish with the dill sprigs.

Serve accompanied by a sauceboat or ramekin of the dill crème fraiche.

CORNERFLAG RESTAURANT
Villa Park, Birmingham B6 6HE
Tel: 0121 326 1519

Rosette of lamb, sweet capsicum and basil stuffing, minted Béarnaise sauce

Lamb

1 double loin of best quality English or Welsh double loin lamb, boned, skinned and defatted

1 red pepper skinned and finely chopped

40g fresh basil leaves

1 shallot and 2 garlic cloves finely chopped and cooked in olive oil

60g fresh white breadcrumbs

1 egg yolk

Salt, fresh mill pepper

75g caul fat (lining of pig's stomach) soaked in cold water

Lamb jus

Bones from double loin chopped. The butcher will do this for you after boning the lamb.

1tbsp tomato purée

200g chopped onion, carrot, leek, and celery

Bay leaf

Garlic clove

Parsley stalks, crushed

Thyme sprig

1 glass red wine (250ml)

1 litre lamb or beef stock

Minted Béarnaise

3 egg yolks

1tbsp water

200g butter

3tbsp chopped mint

2tbsp white wine vinegar

20g chopped shallot

6 crushed peppercorns

Lemon juice

Lamb

Trim off any excess fat from the boned loin without worrying about taking too much off. Season well and lay flat on a chopping board.

Add the chopped capsicum to the cooked shallot and garlic mix, then with the fresh white breadcrumbs followed by the basil finely shredded. Add an egg yolk to bind.

Place stuffing onto opened loin and roll not too tightly so that the stuffing bursts out through cooking.

Cover the rolled loin with the caul fat and then tie gently and refrigerate, whilst other preparation is taking place.

Seal in hot vegetable oil to colour and season. Place in oven at 190°C and cook for 40 minutes. Try to time the cooking of the lamb so that you have at least 20 to 30 minutes for allowing to rest before carving.

Jus

Roast bones through oven until browned with the chopped vegetables. Place bones with vegetables into large saucepan together with the rest of the ingredients and bring to the boil, skim and simmer for one and a half hours.

Strain off jus into clean saucepan and reduce to desired consistency.

Béarnaise sauce

Melt the butter in a small saucepan over low heat.

Put the vinegar, half of the mint, the shallot and crushed peppercorns in a small, heavy-based saucepan. Simmer gently until reduced by half. Remove from the heat and allow to cool.

Add the egg yolks and cold water to the vinegar mixture. Set the pan over low heat and whisk continuously for about five minutes until the sauce emulsifies. Do not allow it to reach boiling point.

Remove the pan from the heat. Whisk in the clarified butter a little at a time. Season to taste, then push sauce through a fine sieve. The Béarnaise should be fairly thick. Stir in remaining mint and lemon juice to taste.

To serve

Carve the lamb into four thick slices into the centre of the serving plate. Ensure the sauce is simmering.

Special note

It may be a nice touch to set the lamb on top of a quenelle of mash, puréed root vegetables or even a potato rosti.

Nape the Béarnaise over the lamb, this should sit on the lamb and then glaze under the grill or with a blow torch.

Ladle the sauce around the lamb and serve.

This dish would be perfectly accompanied with sugar snaps or fine beans and some baby carrots.

CORNERFLAG RESTAURANT
Villa Park, Birmingham B6 6HE
Tel: 0121 326 1519

Blueberry and caramelised apple bread and butter pudding

INGREDIENTS

4 slices of brioche bread or 4 baby brioche rolls.

100g unsalted butter for spreading on brioche

250g punnet of blueberries

1 Bramley apple

50g un-salted butter for cooking apple

50g demerara sugar

4 eggs

2 yolks

300ml double cream

300ml full cream milk

60g vanilla flavoured caster sugar

Icing sugar for dusting

250g pot thick Jersey cream

METHOD

Make up egg custard by beating eggs lightly with caster sugar in a pan or a bowl. Bring the milk and cream gently to the simmer and gradually whisk into the egg mixture and then leave to rest.

Pre-heat grill.

Peel and core apple then slice into segments. Melt butter and brush a flat baking tray, lay out apple and brush with more butter and then sprinkle with the demerara sugar liberally. Place under grill to barely cook, until the sugar caramelises over the apple.

Slice and butter bread and cut each slice into half or quarters depending on size and then layer with the blueberries and apple into a suitable buttered earthenware dish or into individual buttered foil containers if available.

Preheat oven to 140ºC.

Skim any froth off the top of the custard and then pour over the bread and fruit waiting for it to settle and then top up.

Place pudding(s) in larger deep bain-marie roasting tin and place in oven. Individual puddings should take approximately 25 minutes, in the larger dish maybe 45 minutes until golden. Leave to rest.

The individual puddings can be turned out onto plates, dust with icing sugar and serve with thick Jersey cream.

Special note

The individual puddings can be prepared well in advance and chilled, turned out onto a buttered baking dish and reheated gently. This will make the puddings soufflé and turning a golden brown colour.

CORNERFLAG RESTAURANT
Villa Park, Birmingham B6 6HE
Tel: 0121 326 1519

DEL VILLAGGIO

Luciano Canpanella, head chef

DEL VILLAGGIO

Del Villaggio is situated on Broad Street, Birmingham and enjoys one of the best locations in the city. The executive chef Luciano Canpanella, was head-hunted from Italy to bring authentic Italian cuisine to the restaurant.

Luciano prides himself on using only the finest, freshest ingredients to create original, traditional Italian recipes, and he holds three principals very close to his heart:

To create authentic Italian food

To share his passion of the taste of Italy with everybody

To serve his creations in excellent surroundings

At the heart of Del Villaggio is a core lunch and dinner menu developed by Luciano to emphasise the use of Italian cooking methods. There is also a monthly regional menu that explores the diversity of Italy, whether it be Sicily one month or Puglia (home to Luciano) the next.

Most of the ingredients used at Del Villaggio are sourced directly from Italy, from the eight-year-old balsamic vinegar to cherry tomatoes from Sicily and buffalo Mozzerella from Naples. The pizza dough, pasta and ice cream are all home-made to further enhance your culinary experience.

As luciano says about his role: "I give my passion to the cooking and to the business because I believe in it and they believe in me."

Trofiette with rocket pesto and fresh clams

INGREDIENTS

500g trofiette pasta

160g rocket pesto

500g clams

60g white wine

10g garlic

50g olive oil

8 cherry tomatoes to serve

Rocket pesto (for 550g)

200g clean rocket leaves

20g boiled potatoes

20g parsley leaves

20g garlic

60g grated Parmesan

35g Pecorino cheese

45g pine nuts

200g olive oil

4g salt

METHOD

Cook the trofiette pasta in the boiling water for 10 minutes. In the meantime place the olive oil in a saucepan and sauté the garlic with clams for two minutes, add the white wine and reduce it. Add some water and leave the clams to cook for five minutes. When the pasta is ready add to the clams, mix very well and finely add the pesto and mix it without cooking.

Rocket pesto

Place all the ingredients into a blender and mix until very fine.

To serve

Place the trofiette pasta on four plates and place the clams all around the plate. Cut the cherry tomatoes in half and put four halves in the middle of each plate. Dress with pesto.

DEL VILLAGGIO
245 Broad Street, Birmingham B1 2HQ
Tel: 0121 643 4224
www.del-villaggio.com

Stuffed squid with prawns, oysters and vegetables in saffron sauce

INGREDIENTS

5 large squid tubes	**Saffron sauce**
10 prawns	300g fish stock
5 oysters	150g potatoes
1 courgette	100g white wine
1 carrot	1 banana shallot
1 red pepper	1 bag of 125mg saffron
250g cooked spinach	
100g olive oil	
10g garlic	

METHOD

Saffron sauce

Open the oysters and separate the water from the pulp, then add the oyster water in the boiled fish stock and discard from any froth at the top. Strain the stock and add diced potatoes, banana shallot chopped very fine and white wine. Simmer until reduced to half, add the saffron and blend together.

Stuffed squid

Cut all the vegetables, except the spinach, in very thin slices and panfry with olive oil for just five minutes and season with salt and pepper.

Stuff the squid tubes with the vegetables, prawns and oyster (one of each in every squid) and close with a toothpick.

Panfry the squid with olive oil and garlic and let them cook for ten minutes.

Leave the squid to cool down for two to three minutes and then cut them in to three rings.

To serve

Warm the spinach in a sauté pan with a little bit of butter and place it in the middle of five plates. Place the three rings of squid on the top of it and place the saffron sauce all around.

DEL VILLAGGIO
245 Broad Street, Birmingham B1 2HQ
Tel: 0121 643 4224
www.del-villaggio.com

Tiramisu

INGREDIENTS

Tiramisu sauce

5 large fresh eggs
500g mascarpone cheese
75g caster sugar
1tbsp Marsala wine

Tiramisu

300g savoiardi biscuits
275ml espresso coffee
800g tiramisu sauce
20g cacao powder

Basket

3 egg whites
100g caster sugar
100g unsalted butter
100g plain flour

METHOD

Tiramisu sauce

Separate eggs and whisk whites until stiff. Mix very well egg yolks with sugar, add the mascarpone cheese and mix again for five minutes. Mix together both egg mixtures carefully and add the Marsala wine.

Tiramisu

Dip half of the biscuits, one by one, into coffee on both sides very gently and place in a deep dish. Add a third of tiramisu sauce and layer on top of the biscuits. Repeat the procedure with the other biscuits and a third of tiramisu sauce. Keep the other third of the sauce in the fridge to complete the dessert. Place the tiramisu in the fridge and leave it for two hours.

Basket

Mix the ingredients one by one in the same order as listed without whisking too much. Leave in the fridge for half an hour.

Preheat the oven to 180°C. Take a dessertspoon of mixture, place on the baking sheet and spread into a neat round using the back of the spoon. Bake for about seven to eight minutes until golden brown. Lift off with a spatula and put on top of a pudding basin placed upside down. Wrap around a ramekin and press for a couple of minutes until cooled.

To serve

Divide the tiramisu into the baskets and add 1tbsp of the remaining tiramisu sauce on top of each until you use all the mixture.

Place the tiramisu in the middle of the plate and sprinkle with cacao powder.

DEL VILLAGGIO
245 Broad Street, Birmingham B1 2HQ
Tel: 0121 643 4224
www.del-villaggio.com

FINO CAFÉ BAR & RESTAURANT

FINO CAFÉ BAR & RESTAURANT

Fino Café Bar & Restaurant is a stylish, contemporary Italian-themed venue on the waterfront at The Mailbox.

Fino is divided into two distinct areas – the Café Bar, with its attractive summer terrace, and the main restaurant.

Fino Café Bar offers a tempting range of freshly ground Italian coffee, antipasti and light bites as well as a fully licensed bar throughout the day. At night, it becomes a stylish cocktail and wine bar with regular guest DJs and a friendly, funky atmosphere.

Fino Restaurant is a vibrant, buzzing dining room with relaxed, friendly service and a very continental feel. The extensive brasserie style menu and wine list provide heartier fare, with great portions and excellent value. Choose from a selection of meat and fish grills, roasts, pasta and risotto.

Whatever the occasion, Fino is a great place to meet, relax, eat and drink at any time of the day or evening.

Seared scallops with sauce bouillabaisse

4 x red mullet	200g fresh tomatoes halved
100ml olive oil	300g tomato purée
1 pinch saffron	150ml cognac
$1/2$tspn cayenne pepper	150ml Pernod
100g chopped onion	2 litres fish stock
100g chopped carrot	200ml double cream
50g diced potato	
6 cloves garlic	16 large fresh scallops
1 bulb fennel	Salt and pepper to season

Scale and gut the mullet, remove all innards, gills and eyes then cut the fish into large chunks.

In a sauté pan fry the mullet pieces in half the oil with the saffron and cayenne pepper until golden brown.

In a deep saucepan fry the carrot, onion, potato, fennel and garlic until lightly coloured, then add the fresh tomatoes.

Cook slowly until all the liquid has evaporated then add the tomato purée.

Pour over the vegetables the Cognac and Pernod and ignite the alcohol when the flame dies. Add the red mullet and fish stock to the pan.

Simmer gently for an hour, then liquidise all the contents of the pan until fully blended and smooth. Pass the contents through a fine sieve several times.

Place into a clean saucepan and gently heat then add the cream.

Using a hand liquidiser aerate the sauce until frothy, which is then ready to serve.

Finally, quickly sear the seasoned scallops and sit into the bowl or dish, then fleck the froth over the scallops and sauce around.

FINO CAFÉ BAR & RESTAURANT
120-122 Wharfside Street, The Mailbox, Birmingham B1 1RD
Tel: 0121 632 1232

Confit pork belly, seared foie gras, marjoram jus, Pomme Mousseline

INGREDIENTS

2kg pork belly boned and rolled	
1 clove of garlic	
1 small bunch of thyme	
10 litres of duck fat	
2 slices of foie gras	

Pomme Mousseline

250g Ratte potatoes

50g butter

100g double cream

Marjoram jus

500g pork trimmings

100g sliced shallots

100g sliced button mushrooms

1 bottle Madeira

1 litre of veal jus

1 small bunch of marjoram

50g prunes

30g baby capers

12 baby onions

1 head Savoy cabbage

METHOD

Confit the pork belly in the duck fat with the garlic and thyme for 3 hours at 160ºC. Remove from the fat and roll in cling film. Chill.

For the sauce sauté the pork trimmings, shallots and mushrooms until golden brown and add the Madeira. Reduce by half and then add the veal jus. Reduce until sauce consistency and pass.

For the potatoes cook in salted water until tender. Pass through a potato ricer and add the butter and cream.

To serve

Reheat the pork in a hot pan until golden brown. Boil the sauce and add the prunes, capers, onions and marjoram. Sauté the foie gras. Place the pork on a bed of sautéed cabbage topped with the foie gras and pour the sauce around the outside with a little pomme Mousseline.

FINO CAFÉ BAR & RESTAURANT
120-122 Wharfside Street, The Mailbox, Birmingham B1 1RD
Tel: 0121 632 1232

L' assiette chocolate

INGREDIENTS

Ganache
240g chocolate (70% cocoa)
100g butter
120ml water
400ml double cream

Chocolate fondant
220g chocolate (70% cocoa)
100g butter
4 egg yolks
80g rice flour

80g ground almonds
180g caster sugar
4 egg whites

White chocolate ice cream
6 egg yolks
175g caster sugar
300ml milk
300ml double cream
150g white chocolate

Bitter chocolate mousse
375g bitter chocolate (64% cocoa)
150g butter
4 egg yolks
75g sugar
75g semi-whipped cream
4 egg whites
50g sugar

METHOD

You will need an ice cream maker for this recipe.

Ganache
Melt the chocolate and butter together.
Boil the cream and water and whisk on the chocolate mix.
Pour the ganache into a tray and freeze (25mm deep).

Chocolate fondant
Melt the chocolate and butter together and fold in the egg yolks. Fold in the rice flour and almonds.
Whisk the whites and sugar to meringue and fold into the chocolate mix.
Pipe into cutter lined with greaseproof paper until half full, then place 20mm piece of the frozen ganache in the centre and pipe more of the fondant around. Freeze. Cook for 14 minutes at 180°C.

White chocolate ice cream
Bring the milk and cream to the boil and add the white chocolate.
Whisk the egg yolks with the sugar and add the milk mixture.
Cook this custard until it reaches 84°C. Allow to cool and churn in an ice cream maker.

Bitter chocolate mousse
Melt the chocolate and butter and mix together.
Whisk the egg yolks with the sugar to form a ribbon and fold in the chocolate mix.
Fold the semi-whipped cream in to this mix.
Make a meringue with whites and sugar and fold in to the chocolate mix. Chill.

To serve
Place fondant in centre of plate. Cut square of ganache as shown, with quenelle of mousse on top. Place white chocolate ice cream to other side of fondant (right).

FINO CAFÉ BAR & RESTAURANT
120-122 Wharfside Street, The Mailbox, Birmingham B1 1RD
Tel: 0121 632 1232

JONATHANS'
HOTEL AND RESTAURANT

Executive head chef Nick Wheeler

JONATHANS' HOTEL AND RESTAURANT

When Jonathans' opened as a tiny dining room in 1977 there were practically no British restaurants to be found in Britain.

The fabulous traditional regional dishes, sensational puddings and unending larders of sweetmeats, biscuits, chutneys and preserves were almost forgotten. Almost, but not completely.

The great cookery of our past lived on in literature, recipe books and in the homes, farms and fishermen's cottages of the British people.

Jonathans' consulted this treasure trove of tasty delights and recreated them in their Victorian dining rooms.

The restaurant itself has grown in reputation and spread along its hillside, eventually establishing itself as an internationally-acclaimed venue incorporating a luxury hotel and conference centre.

Diners today become immersed in an atmosphere of well being and luxury. Soft music, quiet conversation and the tantalising aroma of good cooking await.

The dining room is in fact a series of rooms with cosy alcoves, lavishly decorated to suit the period.

Today our cuisine is created by executive head chef Nick Wheeler and his team.

Traditional dishes are still present and time-honoured techniques still used, but the recipes are re-worked to give a modern twist with the freshest market ingredients.

Jonathans' reputation continues to flourish as one of the Midlands' oldest and finest restaurants.

Take the virtual tour at www.jonathans-birmingham.com

Rabbit terrine

INGREDIENTS

284ml double cream	**Rocket and hazelnut pesto**
2.2kg rabbit minced	1 clove garlic
seasoning	12 leaves basil
56ml truffle oil	12 leaves rocket
2 onions (finely chopped)	100g hazelnuts
3 cloves garlic (finely chopped)	284ml olive oil
1 pack streaky bacon	
4 eggs	

METHOD

Mix together pesto ingredients in a blender.

Fry off onions and garlic in half amount of truffle oil. When soft add brandy and reduce by half then mix together with eggs, cream, seasoning, remaining truffle oil, the cooked garlic and onions and the brandy reduction. Finally add the rabbit.

Line four large terrine moulds with bacon, ensuring the bacon is pushed into the bottom of the mould and there is enough overlapping to cover the top of the mould. Fill the moulds with rabbit mixture and cover with the bacon that overlapped, and then cover with foil.

Cook in water bath at 350ºC for one and a half hours. When cooked, cover top terrines with a baking tray and weight it down then allow to cool.

To serve

Slice the terrine into four quarter inch slices, arrange slices on top of some fresh leaves and garnish with fine slices of sweet pepper and rocket pesto.

JONATHANS' HOTEL AND RESTAURANT
16 Wolverhampton Road, Oldbury, West Midlands B68 0LH
Tel: 0121 429 3757
www.jonathans-birmingham.com

Rack of pork

INGREDIENTS

1 x 2 bone rack of pork	170ml jus
2 cabbage balls	Butter
200g sliced potatoes	1 onion, sliced
$1/_2$ litre cider and apple juice	Savoy cabbage
Fresh sage	Seasoning

METHOD

Slice potatoes into quarter inch slices, place in dish with seasoning and cider/apple juice mix, cover and cook for 45 minutes at 350°C. Remove potatoes, reduce cooking stock by half then panfry cooked potatoes in butter and then reduced cooking stock until golden. Score back of the pork and season, roast in oven for 30 minutes. To serve, lightly slice back of pork, do not cut all the way through.

Cabbage balls

Reserve outer leaves of cabbage, ensuring they are not damaged. Shred the rest of the cabbage, blanch and refresh.

Panfry the onions with the blanched cabbage and add the sage, then allow the mixture to cool.

Blanch the whole cabbage leaves and cool, then take one leaf and put two tbsp of cabbage and onion mixture onto the leaf and wrap into a ball shape, then wrap in cling film.

When ready to serve, reheat cabbage by placing in steamer or microwave.

Stack the cider potatoes into two piles on a plate. Place one cabbage ball on the plate then slice another cabbage ball in half. Place the rack of pork on the plate with the bones resting on the whole cabbage ball. Place the two halves of cabbage ball next to the rack of pork and add sage gravy, made by reheating jus with fresh sage leaves.

JONATHANS' HOTEL AND RESTAURANT
16 Wolverhampton Road, Oldbury, West Midlands B68 0LH
Tel: 0121 429 3757
www.jonathans-birmingham.com

Jonathans' trifle

INGREDIENTS

Syllabub

$1/_2$ litre double cream

4tbsp caster sugar

$1/_4$ whole nutmeg, grated

$1/_2$tbsp cinnamon

0.071 litre sherry

0.071 litre brandy

Custard

0.5 litre double cream

1 vanilla pod

8 egg yolks

75g caster sugar

Redcurrant Jam

150g redcurrants

$1/_2$ litre stock syrup (600ml water and 450g caster sugar brought to the boil)

5 leaves gelatine

Sponge

0.9kg sugar

0.9kg self-raising flour

0.9kg margarine

12 eggs

METHOD

Syllabub

Whip syllabub ingredients until soft peaks are formed, then add sherry and brandy and whip until cream is firm.

Custard

Bring the cream to the boil with the vanilla pod. Once boiled, pour over the egg yolks and sugar, which have been mixed together. Mix well and return to the pan, stir constantly until the custard coats the back of a spoon.

Redcurrant jam

Bring syrup stock to the boil with the redcurrants, add soaked gelatine, then cool.

Sponge

Mix together ingredients, place in baking tray and cook for two hours at 300ºC.
   Soak in sherry.

To serve

Take a large red wine glass, add sponge which has soaked in sherry to a quarter of the glass, then add a small layer of redcurrant jam. Take warm custard and add to glass until it is half full. Allow custard to cool and set.
   Top with fresh raspberries until custard is covered, then with syllabub.
   Garnish with mint.

JONATHANS' HOTEL AND RESTAURANT

16 Wolverhampton Road, Oldbury, West Midlands B68 0LH

Tel: 0121 429 3757

www.jonathans-birmingham.com

THE LIVING ROOM

Executive chef director John Branagan

THE LIVING ROOM

The Living Room is now synonymous with great food and drink, excellent service and stylish surroundings. It's your neighbourhood restaurant and bar in most cities across Britain, including of course, Birmingham.

The Living Room is a cool, airy piano bar and restaurant, decorated in earthy tones. Described as Manhattan loft with a colonial twist, the aim is to provide quality without exclusivity, and high levels of service without high prices. A casual, fun, relaxing approach to food and drink has been our success for nearly five years.

Frequent menu changes ensure yet more choice and cater directly for our regular customers.

A dedication to wholesome, simple food and quality cocktails is paramount. We are something of a surrogate mother to city centre loft dwellers seeking ballast and comfort food. Chill out, relax and sample the eclectic menu while lounging on curvaceous chocolate-brown leather banquettes and armchairs.

Music is a highlight – the latest sounds from local musicians are interspersed with boogie-woogie and up-beat blues played on a super-stylish white grand piano.

At The Living Room we have a diverse menu that features starters which blend Asian and European influences; stars include Thai vegetable and noodle soup and mussels of the day and duck spring rolls with a shitake salsa. Main courses include grilled lamb cutlets and sea bass fillets with wilted greens, roasted red peppers and beurre blanc. The Home Comforts section of the menu includes old school classics such as steak, ale and mushroom pie and fish and chips with mushy peas and tartar sauce as well as bangers and mash.

Locals can enjoy a long, leisurely New York-style brunch, and those with heartier appetites can choose between a Sunday roast, a selection of salads or sandwiches while reading the Sunday newspapers.

More info available at www.thelivingroom.co.uk

Chargrilled rustic croute with saffron beurre blanc, asparagus, beans and goats' cheese

INGREDIENTS

Saffron beurre blanc

2 saffron strands

1tsp fresh lemon juice

100ml double cream

250g unsalted butter

50 ml dry white wine

2 x 5cm parsley stalks

3 turns fresh ground black pepper

Pinch salt

One bay leaf

Half a shallot

For the asparagus, peas and beans

200g fresh peas, shell on

200g fresh broad beans, shell on

12 medium asparagus spears

8 cherry tomatoes

4 medium shallots

Olive oil

Salt and pepper

To assemble the croute

Cooked beans and peas

4dsp saffron beurre blanc

12 cooked asparagus spears

4 slices of 1cm-thick goats' cheese log

1 clove fresh garlic

4 slices poppy seed bread

4 sprigs of parsley

4dsp olive oil

6 turns of freshly ground black pepper

100g rocket

4tsp French dressing

METHOD

Saffron beurre blanc

Place the white wine, bay leaf, parsley stalks, saffron, black pepper and shallot into a thick bottomed pan, on a medium heat and reduce by two thirds.

Cut the butter into 1cm cubes and store in iced water.

Pass the reduced white wine mixture through a fine sieve into a stainless steel pan, throw the herbs and shallots away and add the cream.

Place the stainless steel pan on a low heat and simmer, add the butter, a chunk at a time, and gently whisk in to the wine reduction until the butter has melted. Repeat this process until all the butter has been used, do not allow this sauce to boil or it will split. Add the lemon juice and salt to taste.

Keep the sauce warm until needed.

Blanching the asparagus, peas and beans

Half fill a medium pan with water add the salt and bring to the boil. Remove the peas and beans from the pods.

Remove the first 3cm from the bottom of the asparagus, peel the stem of the asparagus starting 3cm from the top then tie with string in bundles of six.

Gently place the asparagus into the pan of boiling water and cook for two-three minutes. Remove and place in the iced water. Repeat this step for the beans, boiling for three to five minutes and the peas boiling for two to four minutes then placing in the iced water.

Peel the shallots and cut into 2mm thick rings.

Place a frying pan onto a medium heat for one minute and add the olive oil, shallot rings and sweat for one to two minutes.

When soft, add the peas, beans and cherry tomatoes and sauté for 10 seconds continuously tossing.

Season with salt and fresh ground black pepper, and place the vegetables together in a suitable container.

Method

Cut the bread cross-ways into 1.5cm-thick slices and drizzle each slice with one teaspoon of olive oil and season with one turn of fresh ground black pepper. Grill the bread on the griddle pan for 45 seconds each side, rub each side with raw garlic. Cut the string from the asparagus and drizzle with one dessert spoon of olive oil and season with two turns of fresh ground pepper.

Griddle the asparagus (across the ribs) for 30 seconds to one minute.

Place three spears on a tray, place a slice of goat's cheese across each group of three spears in the centre.

Place the asparagus and goats' cheese under a hot grill for two-three minutes until the cheese browns.

Heat the beans, peas and tomatoes in the microwave for 30 to 45 seconds on full power.

Place the rocket in the centre of the plate and drizzle with French dressing, with the warm croute on top, and the hot peas and beans on top of the croute.

Sit the hot grilled asparagus onto the centre of the croute/beans, drizzle with warm beurre blanc and garnish with parsley.

THE LIVING ROOM
Unit 4, Regency Wharf 2, Broad Street, Birmingham B1 2JZ
Tel: 0870 44 22 539
www.thelivingroom.co.uk

Grilled lamb cutlets, fondant potatoes and sweet onion marmalade

12 lamb cutlets, French trimmed (your butcher will do this)

4 sticks rosemary, each 8cm

8 cloves garlic

Sweet onion marmalade

1dsp demerara sugar

4 large red onions peeled

4 cloves garlic peeled

2dsp olive oil

2dsp balsamic vinegar

1tsp orange marmalade (thick or thin cut)

Pinch salt

5 turns of fresh ground black pepper

50ml red wine

1dsp cranberry sauce

Bay leaf

100ml water (to add in 50ml amounts)

Fondant potatoes

2 baking potatoes

250ml water

1 vegetable stock cube

1 medium stalk thyme

4 turns fresh ground black pepper

25g unsalted butter

1 clove fresh garlic

Red wine sauce

200ml demi glace sauce

1 x 2cm stalk of thyme

1 clove of garlic

100ml red wine

Sweet onion marmalade

Finely slice the onion and crush the garlic into a fine paste. Mix together.

Place a thick-bottomed pan on a low heat and add the oil, onions, garlic, salt, pepper and bay leaf and sweat for five minutes.

Add the sugar, wine, 50ml water and vinegar to the pan and bring to the simmer. Braise for 15 to 20 minutes and add the cranberry sauce and marmalade.

Continue cooking for 10-15 minutes until the onions are soft and all the liquid has evaporated leaving the onions moist. If onions are not soft enough add another 50ml of water and continue cooking.

Remove from the pan and store in a suitable container, (use caution as this mix will be very hot).

Fondant potatoes

Peel the potato and cut in half from top to tail, round off the edges and cut a thin slice from the base.

Peel and chop the garlic. Dissolve the stock cube in the hot water.

Place all the potatoes into a high sided frying/sauté pan. The pan must be just big enough to fit all the potatoes in.

Pour the stock over the potatoes; add the garlic, thyme and ground black pepper.

Brush each potato with a generous amount of soft butter and bring to the boil. Place in a hot oven (180°C) and cook for 15-20 minutes basting continuously with stock

Remove the pan from the oven and allow the potatoes to cool in what remains of the stock.

Preparing the lamb

Place the garlic and a teaspoon of olive oil into an aluminium foil pouch, seal the foil and roast for 10 minutes at 180°C.

Remove from the oven and cool.

Skewer one cutlet with the rosemary stick, leaving 1 cm of rosemary protruding.

Thread one roasted clove of garlic onto the rosemary tight up to the meat, thread one cutlet with the bones facing the same way as the previous one close up to the garlic. Thread one roasted clove of garlic onto the rosemary tight up to the meat and finish off with the final cutlet close up to the garlic.

Red wine sauce

Demi glace is a basic brown sauce that takes a great deal of time to produce, but there are some very good pre-made fresh sauces available from quality supermarkets.

Peel the garlic and roughly chop.

Place the red wine, garlic and thyme into a thick bottomed pan, place the pan on a medium heat and allow the wine to reduce by half. Add your demi glace and simmer for two to three minutes.

Remove the pan from the heat and pass the sauce through a fine sieve into a clean pan to remove the garlic and thyme. Keep the sauce warm.

Assembling the dish

Heat a frying pan until it smokes and add a teaspoon of oil. Season the lamb lightly with salt and fresh ground black pepper.

Seal the lamb in the pan on all sides first and then place into the oven for 15-20 minutes. For the best flavour and texture cook until pink.

Five minutes before the lamb is ready, place the fondant potatoes (in their original pan) back into the oven to re-heat and crisp up

Remove the lamb from the oven and allow to stand for two-three minutes.

Reheat the red wine sauce and adjust the consistency and seasoning if necessary.

Two minutes before serving place the onion marmalade into the microwave for 30 to 45 seconds on full power.

Assemble the dish as shown.

THE LIVING ROOM

Unit 4, Regency Wharf 2, Broad Street, Birmingham B1 2JZ

Tel: 0870 44 22 539

www.thelivingroom.co.uk

Eton mess

Italian meringue

4 egg whites

275g caster sugar

40ml water

To assemble the dish

5dsp whipped cream

2 leaves fresh mint

2 strawberries (half a strawberry for each to garnish)

$\frac{1}{2}$tsp icing sugar

100g mixed berries

$\frac{1}{2}$tsp cocoa powder

6 pieces Italian meringue per person (approx 2-3cm)

Italian meringue

You will need a sugar thermometer to make Italian meringue, available from a good quality catering supplier.

Ensure that the egg whites have no egg yolk in them also at no time must the egg whites come in contact with any grease. Ensure that all equipment is very clean and be careful when using boiled sugar.

Place 200g of sugar into a thick-bottomed pan, add the water and place on a medium heat. Bring to the boil until the thermometer reaches 118°C. Remove any scum from the sugar and prevent sugar crystals by cleaning the insides of the pan with a pastry brush dipped in clean water.

Whilst the sugar is boiling, put the egg whites and the remainder of the sugar into a food processor. Whisk on a medium speed. The whites are ready when they form peaks.

With the mixer still on medium and the sugar at 118°C, slowly add the boiled sugar to the egg whites and continue to mix for one minute.

Spread the meringue onto a sheet of silicon paper.

Place the meringue on a metal tray in a warm oven (130-140°C) for 25 to 35 minutes but do not allow meringue to brown. Remove from the oven and when completely cold break into irregular pieces approximately 2 to 3cm in size.

To assemble

Allow six pieces of meringue per person and place into a medium mixing bowl. Add the mixed fresh berries and the whipped cream. Mix gently together before placing the mix in the centre of a large salad bowl.

Cut the strawberries in half top to tail and place on top in the centre of the dessert.

Top with picked mint and dust lightly with icing sugar and cocoa powder, allowing the dust to settle on the rim of the bowl.

Serve immediately.

THE LIVING ROOM
Unit 4, Regency Wharf 2, Broad Street, Birmingham B1 2JZ
Tel: 0870 44 22 539
www.thelivingroom.co.uk

MACKENZIE'S BAR AND DINING ROOM

*Head chef
Adam Pickett*

MACKENZIE'S BAR AND DINING ROOM

Birmingham's first gastro bar, Mackenzie's Bar and Dining Room brings an attractive new drinking and dining experience to the city, courtesy of three leading lights from the local leisure and business scene.

Situated opposite the wonderfully ornate architecture of Birmingham law courts, the venue offers a superior 'casual gourmet' menu alongside slick table service akin to New York's business district. With deep leather sofas, crisp linen clothed tables, and a classic granite topped bar, Mackenzie's oozes contemporary sophistication yet its rustic colour scheme and diffused lighting create a setting equally suitable for casual drinks or business lunches.

Serious about its commitment to providing quality food throughout the day and evening, the innovative gastro menu has been created by local chef Adam Pickett and offers everything from simple yet satisfying paninis and wraps to imaginative cassoulets and jambalaya. Fresh fish and vegetarian options are always available with a keen emphasis on supporting the best local suppliers.

Alongside this, Mackenzie's presents Birmingham's largest 'by the glass' wine collection, more than 30 prestige labels and all available by the glass thanks to a unique 'le verre de Vin' preservation system. The venue also has partnership agreements with no less than three Grandes Marque Champagne houses and offers an imaginative cocktail list devised by award winner Julian Gibbs.

Confit of duck, forest mushroom and braised cabbage terrine, edged with peach chutney and red onion marmalade

Terrine

1 duck leg

Duck fat (enough to cover duck leg)

25g shitake mushrooms

25g oyster mushrooms

25g chestnut mushrooms

$^1/_4$ Savoy cabbage

15g potatoes

Pinch saffron

400ml brown chicken stock

$1^1/_2$ gelatine leaves

Butter

Iced water

To finish

Peach chutney

$2^1/_2$ peaches

$^1/_4$ apple

25g chopped tomatoes

$^1/_4$ diced onion

1tbsp crushed garlic

1tbsp crushed ginger

$^1/_4$ lime (juiced)

12g brown sugar

Pinch of cinnamon

Pinch of mixed spice

7ml white wine vinegar

Red onion marmalade

$2^1/_2$ sliced red onions

70g brown sugar

25ml white wine vinegar

25ml balsamic vinegar

Truffle oil to serve

Prepare 24 hours in advance.

Terrine

Soak gelatine leaves in iced water for 20 minutes then squeeze out water.
Confit (cook slowly) duck leg in duck fat. Cool legs and pick meat.
Prepare the brown chicken stock. Reduce by half.
Sauté cabbage leaves quickly in butter until just wilted. Sauté wild mushrooms. Season and drain off excess juice.
Square off potatoes then poach in one third of the chicken stock and a pinch of saffron. Reduce remaining chicken stock by half.
Whisk gelatine leaves into reduced stock over iced water until slightly thickened.
Line terrine dish with the larger cabbage leaves then alternately place each ingredient into the mould, spooning the gelatine mix in between each layer. When complete press down on the mould lightly. Wrap in cling film and set for 24 hours.

Peach chutney

Place all the ingredients into a saucepan and slowly cook for about an hour or until the peaches have completely broken up. Season to taste.

Red onion marmalade

Slice red onions and cook for an hour. Add brown sugar, white wine vinegar and balsamic vinegar and cook for another hour. Season to taste.
Dress on a large plate as illustrated (right) and finish by lightly drizzling with truffle oil.

MACKENZIE'S BAR AND DINING ROOM

5 The Citadel, 190 Corporation Street, Birmingham B4 6QD
Tel: 0121 236 4009
www.mackenziesbaranddiningroom.com

Pan-seared fillet of salmon with slow roasted peppers and pak choi

INGREDIENTS

4 x 7-8oz salmon fillets	Pinch of mixed herbs
200g pak choi	Sun-dried tomato oil
4 peppers (mix of red, green and yellow)	Balsamic reduction
	Wild rocket
4tbsp garlic	Vinaigrette
4tbsp olive oil	

METHOD

Pre-roast peppers with olive oil, garlic and herbs slowly for about half an hour at 150ºC.
Pan-fry salmon on both sides, then finish in the oven to your liking.

Balsamic reduction

Reduce balsamic until toffee consistency.

To serve

Work dry sliced pak choi and peppers and dress on the centre of the plate.
Place salmon on top of the pepper mix.
Drizzle balsamic reduction and sun-dried tomato oil around salmon.
Place wild rocket dressed in vinaigrette on top of the salmon and serve.

MACKENZIE'S BAR AND DINING ROOM
5 The Citadel, 190 Corporation Street, Birmingham B4 6QD
Tel: 0121 236 4009
www.mackenziesbaranddiningroom.com

Raspberry and chocolate ganache and berry tartlets

INGREDIENTS

Pastry

125g unsalted butter

60g caster sugar

10ml vanilla essence

175g plain flour

50g cocoa powder

To serve

Mascarpone cream

White chocolate

Milk chocolate

Filling

300ml whipping cream

140g seedless raspberry jam

115g plain dark chocolate

350g raspberries and other summer fruits

25ml Framboise liquer

10g caster sugar

4 sprigs mint

METHOD

Preparation

Pre-heat the oven to 200°C. Sift the flour and cocoa powder. Break up the chocolate. Pick the mint and wash the berries.

Method

Put the butter, sugar and vanilla essence into a bowl and cream together. Add the sifted flour and cocoa powder a bit at a time until a soft dough forms (this can be done in a food processor). Wrap in cling film and chill for at least an hour.

Once the pastry has rested, line four 8x7.5cm tartlet tins with the pastry and bake blind for 12 minutes.

Place 200ml of the cream and half of the jam in a saucepan and bring to the boil, whisking constantly to dissolve the jam.

Remove from the heat and add the chocolate all at once, stirring until it has melted.

Pour into the pastry-lined tartlet tins, shaking gently to distribute the ganache evenly. Chill in the refrigerator for one hour or until set.

Melt the white chocolate and milk chocolate separately and temper the white chocolate only. Add some of the double cream to the milk chocolate to make a chocolate sauce and put to one side until service.

Make a piping bag out of greaseproofed paper and pipe the two chocolate sauces graduating slightly in size and leave to set.

Place the berries in a large shallow bowl. Heat the remaining jam with half the Framboise liqueur over a medium heat until melted and bubbling. Drizzle over the berries and toss to coat.

Divide the berries among the tartlets, piling attractively. Chill until ready to serve.

To serve

Remove the tartlets from the cases and place one on each plate with a quenelle of mascarpone cream on top and a sprig of mint.

Drizzle the chocolate sauces around the plate as shown.

MACKENZIE'S BAR AND DINING ROOM
5 The Citadel, 190 Corporation Street, Birmingham B4 6QD
Tel: 0121 236 4009
www.mackenziesbaranddiningroom.com

MIXATMECHU

Head chef
Steven
Wakeman

MIXATMECHU

The launch of Mix in June 2004 signalled the arrival of a new way to eat and meet in Birmingham. Inspired by the throbbing heartbeat of Europe, this stunning brasserie oozes style and sophistication and has an ambience all of its own.

Set within the award-winning Summerrow development, Mix is an airy, fresh space that's full of personality and exquisite detail. The al fresco dining opportunities have proved popular with professionals in search of a sun-drenched lunch while at weekends we are delighted to welcome the fashionable and the family with equal enthusiasm.

Mix is all about food with the X factor and the menu is designed to inspire and excite. Our extensive brasserie menu includes a selection of seafood including the sensational Mechu Mix Seafood platter and a freshly displayed array of lobster, turbot and good old fish and chips. Classic dishes including roast breast of duck, confit pork belly and Parmesan potato cake are served with finesse alongside more exotic offerings like monkfish in chilli and coconut broth. Make pudding a priority as the Chocolate Pecan Jack Daniels Cake with Jack Daniels Chocolate Sauce is but one of our delectable desserts, made fresh for your enjoyment.

Mix at Mechu, for food with the X factor.

Deep fried goats' cheese with sun-dried cranberry compôte

INGREDIENTS

4 goats' cheese crottin

200g Oriental breadcrumbs

2 eggs

100ml milk

100g flour

Compôte

250g sun-dried cranberries

250ml red wine vinegar

250g demerara sugar

100g redcurrant jelly

2 red onions, diced

50g butter

Zest and juice of one orange

Zest and juice of one lemon

Aged balsamic vinegar to dress

Chervil to garnish

METHOD

Compôte

Melt the butter and sweat the onion. Add the cranberries and stir. Add the red wine vinegar, sugar, redcurrant jelly, zest and juice of orange and lemon. Reduce by half or until quite 'jammy'.

Set aside and refrigerate.

Goats' cheese

Coat the cheese with flour. Mix together the egg and milk. Dip the cheese into this mixture and then into the breadcrumbs. Dip again without the flour, just the egg and milk then the breadcrumbs.

Set aside and refrigerate until ready to deep fry.

To serve

Place the sun-dried cranberry compôte in the middle of each plate. Sit the goats' cheese on top of the compôte and drizzle the aged balsamic vinegar.

MIXATMECHU
47 Summerrow, Birmingham B3 1JJ
Tel: 0121 710 4222
www.summerrow.com   pippa@summerrow.com

Confit of belly pork
with lychee compôte

INGREDIENTS

$^1/_2$ belly pork (ask your butcher to judge quantity for four)

1 litre goose fat

600ml water

To salt the belly pork

50g salt

1tsp five spice powder

Juice and zest of half orange

Juice and zest of half lemon

Juice and zest of whole lime

2 bay leaves

2 deseeded chillies

3 cloves garlic

2 star anise

$^1/_2$ bunch coriander stalks

2.5cm stem ginger

Pinch black pepper

Lychee compôte

1tbsp olive oil

2 tins lychees

1tbsp five spice powder

50g caster sugar

50ml rice wine vinegar

$^1/_2$ sliced onion

3 Szechuan peppercorns

25ml white wine

4 pieces choi sum (Chinese vegetable)

METHOD

Salting the belly pork

Take all of the ingredients and place into a food processor and mix together until broken down. Rub this mixture all over the flesh side of the pork belly, cover and refrigerate for 24 hours.

Confiting the belly pork

Place the pork belly into a deep roasting tray flesh side up and pour in the goose fat to cover it, leaving the salt mixture on the meat. Pour in the water and cook in a low oven (190°C) for three hours or until tender.

When cooked, remove from roasting tray and press between two trays overnight to remove any excess fat. When pressed, remove from refrigerator and cut into squares of four/six portions.

Remove skin carefully with sharp knife, cut into triangles and cook in a high oven (230°C) until crisp.

For the lychee compôte

Sweat the onions, garlic, ginger and five spice in a thick-bottomed pan until softened without colour. Add the Szechuan peppercorns, white wine, vinegar, sugar. Reduce by half and add the tins of lychees. Reduce to a syrup and season to taste.

To serve

Blanch the Chinese greens in hot salted water. Reheat the pork in a roasting dish in the oven and when hot place the hot greens in the centre of each plate. Sit the pork on top. Heat the lychee compôte and spoon over the pork, placing the warmed crackling on top.

MIXATMECHU
47 Summerrow, Birmingham B3 1JJ
Tel: 0121 710 4222
www.summerrow.com   pippa@summerrow.com

Trio of crème brûlée

INGREDIENTS

Vanilla and ginger flavour crème brûlée

300ml double cream

5 egg yolks

2 pieces stem ginger chopped

Caster sugar to taste

Demerara sugar for glazing

$^1/_2$ vanilla pod

4 ramekins

Coconut and lime flavour crème brûlée

150ml double cream

150ml coconut milk

7 egg yolks

Caster sugar to taste

Juice and zest of one lime

Demerara sugar for glazing

4 ramekins

Tia Maria flavour crème brûlée

200ml double cream

5 egg yolks

100ml Tia Maria

Caster sugar to taste

Demerara sugar for glazing

4 ramekins

METHOD

Vanilla and ginger flavour crème brûlée
Heat the double cream in a thick-bottomed saucepan. Split the vanilla pod and add to the cream.

In a separate bowl beat the egg yolks. Once the cream is heated pour onto the egg yolks stirring constantly. Place bowl over simmering pan of water, add ginger and continue to stir until the mixture becomes quite thick and custard-like. Add sugar to taste. Remove from heat and pour into the four separate ramekins and refrigerate until set. Spread the top of each brûlée with demerara sugar and glaze with a blowtorch.

Tia Maria flavour crème brûlée
Use the same method as for the vanilla, but add the Tia Maria to the double cream once heated.

Coconut and lime flavour crème brûlée
Mix the coconut milk and double cream together with the lime juice and zest. Heat and repeat as for vanilla and ginger method.

To serve
Sprinkle a thin layer of demerara sugar on the top of each brûlée and caramelise with a blowtorch. Place a selection of the three brûlée on the centre of each plate and decorate with summer berries and a vanilla pod. Serve with a dusting of icing sugar.

MIXATMECHU
47 Summerrow, Birmingham B3 1JJ
Tel: 0121 710 4222
www.summerrow.com   pippa@summerrow.com

MIYAKO TEPPANYAKI

Kiran Chauhan

MIYAKO TEPPANYAKI

Teppanyaki is a unique culinary art that has established itself as one of the favourites of Japanese cuisine, its preparation and presentation take place before your eyes on a heated steel plate.

The minimalism that exists in Japanese aesthetics is also evident in the culinary culture, whether it be in the taste, flavour, presentation or in the cooking itself.

At Miyako Teppanyaki our specially trained chefs will delight the gourmet guests with their individual cooking and artistic skills – it is real theatre, especially when the chefs use white wine and brandy to flambé the food.

The restaurant itself is very well-established with a history going back some 14 years – it was the first in "China Town", the Arcadian Centre and the first Japanese restaurant in Birmingham.

Both the interior and signage reflect the colours of the Japanese flag, red and white, whilst inside it is a classic linear design with screens, black leather and ivory walls.

We aim to create a feel of Japan in the heart of Birmingham, with a private atmosphere to take you away from it all.

Using the freshest ingredients, our chefs introduce the food to you course by course and explain what they are doing at each stage.

A nice finish to the meal is a cup of traditional Japanese green tea – or perhaps even some of our homemade green tea ice cream.

To accompany the dishes we have all the top branded Japanese beers, Sake (Japanese rice wine), and a large variety of Champagne including Cristal, Krug and Laurent Perrier – which prove very popular for the large number of birthday parties we host here at Miyako.

Kiran Chauhan,
Miyako Group Limited

Mussel shells filled with shredded crabmeat and mussel with plum wine sauce and deep fried parsley

INGREDIENTS

12 pieces large New Zealand mussels
Shredded crab meat (you can use crabsticks if you cannot get crab meat)

Plum wine sauce

Butter

Crushed clove garlic

50ml plum wine

Salt and pepper for seasoning

Fresh parsley, deep fried and crumbled

METHOD

Remove mussel meat from the shell. Clean the shells, as they will be used for serving.
Steam the mussel meat for five minutes, shred the crab meat finely.
For the sauce, melt butter, add the garlic, plum wine, salt and pepper.
In the mussel shells place some shredded crab meat, once steamed place the mussel meat on top of the crab meat, then drizzle plum wine sauce, and finish off with deep fried parsley for decoration.

MIYAKO TEPPANYAKI

China Town, Arcadian Centre, Ladywell Walk, Hurst Street, Birmingham B5 4ST
Tel: 0121 622 5183

Yasai tempura

A selection of mixed vegetables, sliced, dipped into a light tempura batter, seasoned and then deep fried into balls, served with ginger and daikon (white radish) sauce.

INGREDIENTS

A handful of a selection of vegetables – carrots, beansprouts, aubergine, red/green peppers, sweet potato, onion, green beans

Tempura batter

Tempura flour (available from most Oriental stores)

Ice cold water

1 egg yolk

Tempura sauce (to dip)

1ml mirin

5ml dashi water

25ml soy sauce

1 tsp finely grated ginger

1 tsp finely grated daikon (white radish)

METHOD

Batter

Mix the ingredients together in a bowl until a light batter consistency. Use roughly one cup of flour to one cup of water; you are looking for the same kind of consistency as chip shop batter.

Slice all the vegetables into thin stripes.

Roll the sliced vegetables in tempura flour so that they are lighly coated, add a pinch of salt and pepper, then place in the tempura batter mixture.

Heat oil, when hot with a long tablespoon place the mixture one by one into the hot oil. Fry until golden brown in colour.

Tempura sauce

Mix all the ingredients together and use as dipping sauce.

MIYAKO TEPPANYAKI
China Town, Arcadian Centre, Ladywell Walk, Hurst Street, Birmingham B5 4ST
Tel: 0121 622 5183

Beef Ozuyaki

Thinly sliced stripes of sirloin steak, stuffed with garlic, mushroom, and spring onion, the stripes are then rolled with the stuffing and cooked in Tokyo butter sauce and sake (Japanese rice wine).

INGREDIENTS

For each roll, 5/6 stripes of sirloin steak

Finely chopped mushroom, spring onion, and two cloves garlic

Butter

1tsp oil (olive or sesame seed)

Brandy for flambaying

Tokyo butter sauce

Butter

Soy sauce

Pepper, white pepper if available

Sake

METHOD

Place a tea spoon of oil into a large frying pan, add finely chopped garlic, mushrooms, spring onions and fry until slightly brown.

Place another teaspoon of oil in another pan, then place the sirloin stripes of beef so that they are overlapping each other. Once the meat has seared place the garlic, mushroom and spring onion stuffing in the centre, then gently roll the meat with two flat spatulas. Once rolled, add small amount of brandy and light for flambé.

Tokyo butter sauce

Melt the butter then mix rest of the ingredients. Pour over the ozuyaki roll.

MIYAKO TEPPANYAKI

China Town, Arcadian Centre, Ladywell Walk, Hurst Street, Birmingham B5 4ST
Tel: 0121 622 5183

PRANA RESTAURANT & LOUNGE

Artist's impression of Prana Restaurant & Lounge, due to open at time of press

*Head chef
Lawson
Shuttleworth*

PRANA RESTAURANT & LOUNGE

A love of international travel was the creative spark for Prana, the owner inspired to open a restaurant in the UK after eating in some of the best restaurants in the world's greatest cities.

We chose Birmingham as it is the most vibrant and culturally exciting city with a flourishing restaurant scene.

Attention to detail is our mantra, with an eclectic menu using the freshest ingredients and global cooking techniques, creating an emphasis on healthy yet tasty eating.

Head chef Lawson Shuttleworth has created a menu full of variety which features such dishes as Côte de Boeuf, Millefeuille of Salmon and Crab, Caviar, Lobster and Oyster as well as more traditional dishes such as Cumberland Sausage and Mash, Coq au Vin and Moussaka.

Vegetarians are also well catered for with many main course choices including pearl barley risotto and lavender and goats' cheese salad.

We believe cooking is like love – it should be entered into with abandonment or not at all!

Christophe Benedetti
General Manager

Seared foie gras with Szechuan pepper, buttered brioche and red onion marmalade

INGREDIENTS

Foie gras

8 slices foie gras

Salt

Szechuan pepper

Buttered brioche

500g strong white flour

5 eggs

225g unsalted butter

75g yeast

150ml milk

75g sugar

Pinch salt

Red onion marmalade

4 red onions

150g soft brown sugar

150g red wine vinegar

150ml red wine

3tbsp balsamic vinegar

Olive oil

METHOD

Foie gras

Pan fry in a small amount of very hot oil for 30 seconds on each side. Season well.

Buttered brioche

Sieve flour into mixing bowl. Sprinkle in sugar and pinch of salt.

Warm milk to room temperature and add yeast and melted butter. Pour ingredients into flour mix until smooth. Add eggs, one at a time, until completely mixed in.

Leave in bowl to prove, (it will double in size). Mould into required shape and once again leave to prove. Put in pre-heated oven at 200°C/400°F for approximately 20 minutes. Place on a cooling tray and serve warm.

Red onion marmalade

Slice the red onions and sweat off in lightly oiled pan until translucent. Add the brown sugar and caramelise down. Add red wine and red wine vinegar. Turn down heat and simmer until all liquids are totally reduced to a sticky consistency. Remove from heat, season, add balsamic vinegar. Leave to cool before serving.

PRANA RESTAURANT & LOUNGE
121 Suffolk Street (located by The Mailbox), Birmingham B1 1LX
Tel: 0121 616 2211
www.pranarestaurant.co.uk

Duck breast, roasted parsnip, sweet potato & pak choi, cinnamon and cassis sauce

INGREDIENTS

Grind together to make herb powder:

8 juniper berries

1 pinch chilli powder

3 star anise

Salt and pepper

$1/_4$ cinnamon stick

4 cardamom pods

4 duck breasts

3 medium size parsnips

3 medium size sweet potatoes

1 clove of garlic

25ml créme de cassis

$1/_4$tsp ground cinnamon

300ml reduced beef stock

1 sprig of thyme

Bunch pak choi

METHOD

Trim fat on duck breasts, season with the herb powder, cover and refrigerate for 24 hours.

Peel and dice parsnips and sweet potato into quarter inch squares. Add to a heated roasting tray with a little olive oil, season then add chopped garlic and sprig of thyme. Roast until just cooked.

Heat a large pan with olive oil, pan fry the duck breasts skin side down, do not colour too much, turn them to seal and cook to taste. Place in oven until required.

Chop up the pak choi, sauté in olive oil, season.

Heat up cassis and cinnamon in a pan, reduce, add beef stock, reduce and season. Present and serve and garnish with deep fried leek strips.

PRANA RESTAURANT & LOUNGE
121 Suffolk Street (located by The Mailbox), Birmingham B1 1LX
Tel: 0121 616 2211
www.pranarestaurant.co.uk

Bitter chocolate and honeycombed tart, coffee bean posit

Bitter chocolate tart

Sweet paste

725g plain flour

25g cocoa powder

(bind together)

375g soft butter

300g icing sugar

2 eggs

3 egg yolks

(bind together)

Bitter chocolate filling

175g unsalted butter

200g dark bitter chocolate

2 eggs

60g caster sugar

4tbsp water

Honeycomb

75g clear honey

140g liquid glucose

400g caster sugar

4tbsp cold water

15g bicarbonate

Coffee bean posit

110g ground coffee beans

250g caster sugar

600ml cream

Bitter chocolate tart

Bind each mixture separately as suggested above. Slowly add together until smooth.

Roll out, place in an eight inch pastry ring. Bake at 200°C/400°F for 20 minutes than leave to cool.

Bitter chocolate filling

Melt the chocolate and butter in a bowl over a pan of simmering water. Whisk eggs until light and fluffy.

Boil the water with the sugar, remove to cold bowl. Whisk eggs into sugar/water mix.

Pour in chocolate mix and fold ingredients together.

Pour into tart case. Refrigerate.

Honeycomb

Heat all of the ingredients, except the bicarbonate, in a large pan until caramelised.

Remove from heat, whisk in bicarbonate.

Pour mixture onto grease proof paper, leave to cool.

Break into pieces to serve with tart.

Coffee bean posit

Boil all ingredients in a pan. Reduce by half. Place in a plastic container, cool then freeze. Serve with tart.

PRANA RESTAURANT & LOUNGE
121 Suffolk Street (located by The Mailbox), Birmingham B1 1LX
Tel: 0121 616 2211
www.pranarestaurant.co.uk

RED PEPPERS

RED PEPPERS

Red Peppers Birmingham opened its doors in March of 2004, and is sister restaurant to the ever popular Bar Estilo in the prestigious Mailbox development.

The menu is eclectic and has developed as a direct result of customers' changing tastes and trends over the past decade since the opening of the first Red Peppers in Teddington, back in the early nineties.

The feel of the restaurant is very Mediterranean and the menu reflects this with dishes such as Bouillabaisse (classic fish stew from Marseille) and Moussaka with Greek salad and flat bread. There are also flavours of North Africa with Tajine style lamb shank served with apricot cous cous and merguez sausage (spiced lamb sausage) with tabbouleh and mint & yoghurt dressing.

Red Peppers strives to offer choices to suit all tastes and as such makes an ideal venue for all occasions. We have also catered for a number of larger parties in our basement restaurant with its own bar where we have created bespoke buffet menus and dinner menus for that special occasion.

Red Peppers looks forward to the same support and welcome that the people of Birmingham so kindly gave us in the early days at Bar Estilo.

Colette Whelan,
Operations director

Warm goats' cheese with caramelised pear and pine nuts

INGREDIENTS

4 circles of goats' cheese (about 1$\frac{1}{2}$cm thick)

4 pieces of focaccia bread cut to the size of the goats' cheese

200g baby leaf salad (or preferred leaves)

1 stick celery cut into thin batons

Handful pine nuts

Caramelised pears

50g caster sugar

Dash lemon juice

25g unsalted butter

2 pears cut into four to six pieces

Dressing

125ml olive oil

50ml clear honey

100ml balsamic dressing

Fresh pepper to taste

METHOD

Caramelised pears

Peel and core the pears. Melt the butter in a frying pan, add sugar and cook until it starts to caramelise.

Add the lemon juice and then the pears and cook slowly until the pears are starting to soften. Remove from the pan and cool.

Dressing

Whisk all ingredients together.

Salad

Preheat grill. Place the pine nuts on a baking tray and toast until golden. Allow to cool.

Combine the leaves, pears and celery in a bowl and drizzle with the honey dressing. Toss the salad in the dressing.

Place the bread on a baking tray and toast lightly on both sides. Place the goats' cheese on top and return to the grill. Cook for a few minutes until the cheese is nicely browned and just starting to melt.

To serve

Divide the dressed salad between four plates. Carefully place the goats' cheese on the top. Drizzle the goats' cheese with a little more of the dressing and sprinkle with the toasted pine nuts.

RED PEPPERS
117 Wharfside Street, The Mailbox, Birmingham B1 1RF
Tel: 0121 643 4202

Tajine style lamb shanks with apricot & raisin cous cous

INGREDIENTS

4 lamb shanks

50ml oil

250g onions (peeled and sliced)

250g potatoes (peeled and cut into 2cm pieces)

175g carrots (peeled and sliced)

4 cloves garlic (crushed)

1.5 litre vegetable stock

1 cinnamon stick

$1^1/_2$tsp turmeric

1tbsp cumin

1 tin chickpeas

2tsp salt

2tsp black pepper

150g dried apricots

75g clear honey

1 bunch coriander

Cous cous

250g cous cous

300ml vegetable stock

1 stick cinnamon

$1^1/_2$tsp turmeric

1tsp cumin

2tsp salt

2tsp black pepper

100g dried apricots (roughly chopped)

50gr raisins

1 bunch coriander

50ml olive oil

METHOD

Heat the oil in a roasting tin. Add the shanks and brown on all sides. Remove the lamb and add the onions and garlic. Cook for five minutes but do not brown.

Place the lamb in a large casserole with the onions, stock, cinnamon, cumin, turmeric, salt and pepper and cover. Cook in the centre of the oven at 180°C until the lamb is tender.

Add the potatoes and carrots and return to the oven until the carrots and potatoes are almost cooked. Add the apricots, chickpeas and honey and cook for a final 15 minutes.

Remove the excess fat from the lamb shanks. Stir in the coriander to make a sauce. Keep to one side to serve with the cous cous.

Cous cous

Bring the stock to the boil with all the spices and seasoning. Simmer for five minutes.

Remove from the heat and add the apricots and raisins.

Add the cous cous and mix well. Leave to stand for five minutes.

Add the oil and mix well to break up the cous cous. Stir in the coriander.

To serve

Place the cous cous in the centre of the plate. Carefully place the lamb shanks against the cous cous and spoon some sauce over the top. Serve any extra sauce separately.

RED PEPPERS
117 Wharfside Street, The Mailbox, Birmingham B1 1RF
Tel: 0121 643 4202

Baked cheesecake with strawberry and mint salsa

INGREDIENTS

250g mascarpone

250g ricotta cheese

1 lemon (juice and rind)

250ml double cream

4 eggs

200g caster sugar

200g Scotch shortcake fingers

50g melted butter

Strawberry and mint salsa

250g strawberries

6 sprigs mint

2tbsp caster sugar

50ml water

METHOD

Mix the ricotta, mascarpone, lemon juice and rind, cream, eggs and sugar together and leave to stand for an hour.

Grind the biscuits to coarse crumbs and add the melted butter. Grease a deep springform cake tin with butter and add the biscuit mix, press into the bottom of the tin.

Stir the cheesecake mix and pour onto the biscuit base.

Place in a preheated oven 150°C for one hour until the top is browning. Turn off the oven and leave for a further 20 minutes.

Remove from the oven and cool. Then refrigerate until completely cold and firm.

Strawberry and mint salsa

Remove the stalks from the strawberries and cut each strawberry into six to eight pieces. Place half of the strawberries in a small saucepan with the sugar and 50ml water. Bring to the boil and simmer until the strawberries are soft.

Remove from the heat and press the strawberries through a sieve so you have a smooth sauce. Allow to cool.

Chop the mint leaves and mix with the remaining strawberries. Once cool add the sauce and mix well.

To serve

Place a piece of cheesecake in the centre of the plate and spoon the salsa over the top.

RED PEPPERS
117 Wharfside Street, The Mailbox, Birmingham B1 1RF
Tel: 0121 643 4202

SANCTUM

Head chef
Staale Ellevsen

SANCTUM

We first developed the idea of Sanctum in the summer of 2001. Our aim was to create a place where you would feel at home whether you were taking time out from the office or having a social get-together.

We combined our unique experiences of having eaten, trained or worked in some of the world's most prestigious restaurants to create something that went beyond just food. This is when we came up with 'discover your senses'.

Nestling at the foot of a spiral staircase is an elegant, modern and relaxing hideaway, Sanctum. Our menu takes fresh ingredients and creative ideas from around the world, and our internationally sourced wine list always provides the ideal accompaniment.

What Sanctum genuinely excels at is being a place where you feel comfortable whether you're entertaining clients or relaxing with friends. We believe that it is the little things that make the difference.

You've discovered Sanctum, now discover your senses.

Joel and Staale

Butterfly shrimp with Creole sauce

INGREDIENTS

4 large shrimps	1 clove of garlic finely chopped
1 egg	5 black olives finely chopped
2tbsp milk	$^1/_4$ de-seeded red chilli finely chopped
2tbsp of any wheat flour	$1^1/_2$tbsp whole grain mustard
30g panko (Japanese honey bread crumbs)	100ml tomato juice
	Salt and pepper to taste
2 plum tomatoes skinned and diced	35g rocket
1 medium shallot diced	

METHOD

Peel the shrimp and de-vein. This is done by scoring along the outside edge of the shrimp tail to within 1.5cm of the tail, to reveal a string-like substance that can easily be removed. Lightly beat the egg and milk together.

Roll the shrimp in the flour and then in the lightly beaten egg and milk. Coat the shrimp in the breadcrumbs. Fry in vegetable oil at 175°C for two minutes.

Sauce

Sweat off the shallots and garlic in a pan. Add the plum tomatoes, olives, chillies, whole grain mustard and tomato juice. Cook for around 15 minutes. Add salt and pepper according to your taste.

To serve

Place the shrimps on a bed of rocket. Drip the sauce around the edge of the bed of rocket.

SANCTUM
110 Colmore Row, Birmingham B3 3AG
Tel: 0121 236 1110
www.sanctumbirmingham.com

Coconut Thai chicken

INGREDIENTS

200g chicken breast, skinned and boneless

Paste

20g fresh coriander

$^1/_4$ green chilli

10g fresh ginger

20g spring onion

10g garlic

15g lemongrass

40ml Thai fish sauce

Garnish

10g yellow pepper thinly sliced

10g red pepper thinly sliced

10g green pepper thinly sliced

15g spring onion thinly sliced

$^1/_4$ red chilli thinly sliced

300ml coconut milk

1 pack of pre-cooked egg noodles

METHOD

Place the chicken breast, with what was the skin side down. With a sharp knife make a 1cm deep incision along the length of the breast. Then lie your knife horizontally on the breast and carefully cut out until the blade of the knife is 1cm from the edge of the breast. Spin the breast 180° and repeat. The breast will now be opened up into an almost oval shape.

Put all ingredients for the paste in a blender and blend very well.

Put the opened chicken breast on a 450mm x 450mm sheet of cling film. Add three tablespoons of the paste onto the chicken. Roll the chicken with the cling film into a tightly wrapped cylindrical shape so that the cling film forms a tight skin around the chicken. Ensure that the ends are tightly sealed. Cook in simmering water for approximately 20 minutes.

Next, heat the coconut milk in a pan and unwrap the chicken over the coconut milk allowing the juices to fall into the pan. Set the chicken aside. Add the thinly sliced garnish ingredients and pack of pre-cooked egg noodles to the coconut milk and allow to simmer. While the noodles and vegetables are simmering slice along the chicken roll at 1cm intervals to create a fan effect.

To serve

Place the noodles and vegetables in a deep plate and with the chicken sitting on top.

SANCTUM

110 Colmore Row, Birmingham B3 3AG

Tel: 0121 236 1110

www.sanctumbirmingham.com

Truffle torte

Serves 8

INGREDIENTS

100g Amaretti biscuits

600g dark chocolate (75% cocoa solids chocolate)

7tbsp liquid glucose

7tbsp dark rum

750ml double cream (room temperature)

METHOD

Finely crush the Amaretti biscuits and sprinkle them into a 25cm cake tin. Put it in the fridge. Melt the chocolate adding the rum and glucose when the chocolate has fully melted. Set aside for five minutes. Whip the cream until it thickens slightly. Add half of the cream to the chocolate mixture, and mix well. Then fold the chocolate mixture into the rest of the cream making sure that they are well mixed. Carefully pour the mixture into the cake tin with the crushed biscuits in. Cover with cling film and leave in the fridge overnight.

Take a small knife and run it around the edge of the cake tin. Turn the cake upside down onto a serving plate and remove the tin. The biscuit crust will now be on top.

Serve with a fruit coulis and a shot of good frozen whisky.

SANCTUM
110 Colmore Row, Birmingham B3 3AG
Tel: 0121 236 1110
www.sanctumbirmingham.com

SIMPLY SIMPSONS

*Head chef
Iain Miller*

SIMPLY SIMPSONS

Simply Simpsons is the new sister restaurant of Simpsons Birmingham.

Having been home to the original Simpsons in Kenilworth for 11 years, the site has been extensively refurbished and rebranded to serve as a fresh, new Simpsons experience.

Simplicity is key to the Kenilworth venture with the accent on simpler, quality cuisine in a relaxed environment.

Simpsons built up an impressive reputation in the locality and beyond, and it is from this firm footing that Simply Simpsons plans to strike forth with something a little different to offer.

The accent moves to a slightly more laid back feel, with the standard of cuisine intact within a great new setting.

For those who loved the flair of the Simpsons menu, there will be plenty of reminders mingling amidst new ideas. Head chef Iain Miller plans to include a few of the favourite dishes from the original Simpsons menu such as Slow Braised Shank of Lamb and Bavette of Beef with Red Wine Shallots. Other dishes will include Potato Pancake, Smoked Salmon and Sauce Vert, Black Pudding and Poached Egg Salad and desserts such as, Vanilla Crème Brûlée and Chocolate Tart.

The Simpsons faithful are to be welcomed back with open arms to Simply Simpsons, along with a new clientele attracted no doubt by a combination of curiosity and the prestigious presence of Simpsons in Birmingham.

Orso with crab, chilli and pesto

INGREDIENTS

	Pesto
150g Orso pasta	**Pesto**
1 mild red chilli	Small bunch basil
200g picked crab meat	100g pine nuts
70g Gremolata (see below)	1 clove garlic (peeled)
Salt	50g Parmesan (grated)
Butter	100ml olive oil
Seasoning	
50g rocket salad	

Parmesan shavings to serve

METHOD

Gremolata is basically 100g parsley leaves, the zest of two lemons, 1 crushed clove of garlic and 100ml olive oil, whizzed up in a blender for two minutes.

Cook the Orso in boiling salted water until soft. Deseed and wash the red chilli and chop finely. Place a small knob of butter in a saucepan and place on a medium heat. Add the chilli to the pan as it starts to bubble and cook. Add the Gremolata when hot and add the Orso and crab meat plus rocket. Stir to mix, season with salt and pepper and serve with pesto, made by blitzing the above ingredients.

SIMPLY SIMPSONS
101-103 Warwick Road, Kenilworth, Warwickshire CV8 1HL
Tel: 01926 864567
www.simpsonsrestaurant.co.uk

Beef and bones with chips

INGREDIENTS

4 fillet steaks, 9oz on the bone

4 very large Maris Piper potatoes

Seasoning

Butter

METHOD

We like to shape chips as small bananas, but you can do conventional chips if you prefer. When peeled and shaped, soak in cold water for five minutes. Transfer the chips to a pan, cover with salted water and par boil for five minutes and drain.

The potatoes should have a slightly sticky feel to them, which will help them crisp.

Submerge the chips into a pan of frying oil at 100°C until cooked through. Remove and allow to cool. Turn up frying oil heat to 190°C.

Ensure the pan is hot and seal the steaks for two minutes each side, longer if you want them cooked more. Season with salt and pepper and put a large knob of butter in the pan.

Put the chips back into the hot frying oil for three to four minutes until golden and crisp. Serve.

SIMPLY SIMPSONS
101-103 Warwick Road, Kenilworth, Warwickshire CV8 1HL
Tel: 01926 864567
www.simpsonsrestaurant.co.uk

Prune and Armagnac ice cream and espresso syrup

Prunes

500g Agen prunes

250g sugar

Water to cover

2 Earl Grey teabags

1 cinnamon stick

1 vanilla pod

2 star anise

2 cloves

Armagnac ice cream

250ml cream

250ml milk

100ml Armagnac

6 egg yolks

175g sugar

Espresso syrup

200ml coffee

300g sugar

You will need an ice cream maker for this dish.

Prunes

This needs to be prepared a day in advance.

Place all ingredients in a large pan, slowly bring to the boil over a low heat and simmer for ten minutes. Place prunes in a bowl and cover, leaving to infuse overnight.

Armagnac ice cream

Cream together the yolks and sugar, boil the cream milk and Armagnac together and pour over the creamed yolks whilst whisking. Allow mix to cool and churn in an ice-cream maker.

Espresso syrup

Boil the sugar with just enough water to cover, until softball stage (240°F) is reached. Mix in warmed coffee and chill.

SIMPLY SIMPSONS
101-103 Warwick Road, Kenilworth, Warwickshire CV8 1HL
Tel: 01926 864567
www.simpsonsrestaurant.co.uk

SIMPSONS

Head chef
Luke Tipping

SIMPSONS

Birmingham gained its first Michelin starred restaurant with the arrival of Simpsons in leafy Edgbaston.

The restaurant moved from Kenilworth to a beautiful Georgian Grade II listed building.

In these splendid surroundings, with the benefit of four ensuite bedrooms above, chef patron Andreas Antona is developing his fine dining restaurant, taking it to higher levels of excellence.

Simpsons enjoys the unique location of the Calthorpe Estate. One of Britain's largest urban conservation areas, it comprises a stunning collection of Georgian villas and grand leafy gardens. The restaurant has lovely garden views and an orangery, making it hard to believe that the restaurant is just one mile from the city centre of Birmingham.

Inside Simpsons, the main dining room seats 70 people, with a separate bar and lounge area for pre and post dinner drinks. A beautiful high ceilinged and naturally-lit private dining room accommodates up to 20 guests.

Guests wishing to extend their gourmet visit will be able to choose from four luxurious bedrooms each designed in the differing themes of French, Venetian, Colonial and Oriental.

In close collaboration with head chef Luke Tipping, Andreas presents light, modern dishes based on classical French cuisine. Typical dishes from the à la carte menu include starters such as Ravioli of Scallop with Truffled Chicken Jus and Seared Foie Gras, Pain d'Epice and Citrus Fruits. Main courses include such delights as Roast Saddle and Slow-Braised Shoulder of Cornish Lamb with Aromatic Couscous, Pan-Fried Daurade with Potato Scales and Sevruga Caviar Sauce. Desserts that are hard to resist include Mille-feuille of Turron Parfait, Caramelised Banana and Caramel Sauce and Chilled Coconut Rice Pudding.

Simpsons is open for lunch and dinner, seven days a week.

Seared scallop, sesame crust and endive marmalade

INGREDIENTS

Fresh scallops must be used

12 scallops

50g sesame seeds

1tbsp vegetable oil

Seasoning

1 egg white

4 portions sauce Epice

4 portions endive marmalade

Sauce Epice

100ml white wine vinegar

150ml red wine vinegar

200g brown sugar

3 star anise, 10g coriander seeds, 10g pink peppercorns, 10g fennel seeds, all blitzed in a food processor for 1 minute

Endive marmalade

5 heads chicory

2 large shallots

25g sherry vinegar

25g white wine vinegar

20g butter

$1/_2$tsp salt

3tsp sugar

Pinch ground black pepper

METHOD

Scallops

Lay out 12 scallops on a flat tray. Brush the top of the scallops with egg white and dip them into the sesame seeds, ensuring just to cover the tops of the scallops.

Heat oil in a flat frying pan and seal the scallops, sesame crust side first. Cook for two minutes, ensuring not to catch, and flip them carefully over and cook for a further minute. Take from heat and serve.

Sauce Epice

Put all ingredients together in a pan and bring to the boil. Reduce to a syrup that sticks to the back of a spoon.

Endive marmalade

Shred shallots and sweat off in butter. Shred chicory and add to shallots. Add both vinegars, salt, sugar and pepper and simmer until all fluid has evaporated and marmalade consistency achieved.

SIMPSONS
20 Highfield Road, Edgbaston, Birmingham B15 3DX
Tel: 0121 454 3434
www.simpsonsrestaurant.co.uk

Roast Gressingham duck, pak choi, glazed apple, celeriac purée, honey and cracked pepper sauce

INGREDIENTS

1 Gressingham duck

1 apple

1 celeriac

2 pak choi

1 pint duck fat

100ml honey and cracked pepper sauce

1tbsp sugar

Milk (enough to cover)

Honey and cracked pepper sauce

2tsp honey

6 crushed peppercorns

100ml veal glace

METHOD

Remove the legs from the duck and confit (cook slowly) in the duck fat at 90-100°C for two and a half hours or until tender.

Remove the duck breasts and put skin side down into a cold frying pan and then put onto a medium heat. The breasts will release a lot of fat so keep draining it off until the skin browns and crisps. Then roll the breasts over and cook in the oven at 200°C for two minutes on the flesh side.

Rest the breasts for four to five minutes but turn the breast every minute. If you want your duck breast cooked further, leave in oven for an extra couple of minutes before resting.

Celeriac purée

Peel and chop the celeriac. Put in pan and cover with equal amounts of water and milk with a pinch of salt. Boil and simmer until soft and breaking up. Remove from pan and drain. Blitz in a blender for two minutes or until puréed.

Peel and cut apple, place in a small bowl with 25g of butter and a pinch of sugar. Cover with cling film and place in a microwave for one minute on full power.

Cut the root from the pak choi and separate the leaves and wash them. Blanch in boiling salted water for 30 seconds.

Honey and cracked pepper sauce

Add all ingredients together, bring to the boil and serve as shown.

SIMPSONS
20 Highfield Road, Edgbaston, Birmingham B15 3DX
Tel: 0121 454 3434
www.simpsonsrestaurant.co.uk

Rum baba, exotic fruits and crème Chantilly

INGREDIENTS

Baba

100ml warm milk

15g fresh yeast

Pinch salt

230g soft flour

3 whole eggs

125g soft butter

Apricot jam

Exotic fruits

1 pineapple

1 mango

1 papaya

2 kiwi

200g caster sugar

300ml water

1 cinnamon pod

1 vanilla pod

1 star anise

Chantilly

250ml double cream

1 vanilla pod

30g icing sugar

Rum liquor

300ml water

300ml rum

120g sugar

METHOD

Baba

Dissolve the yeast into the milk. Sieve the flour and salt into a mixing bowl and add the milk mixture and eggs to form a smooth dough and add the softened butter. Prove, place into small ramekin moulds, reprove and bake at 200°C for eight minutes. When cool coat in apricot jam.

Exotic fruits

Infuse cinnamon, vanilla and anise. Boil with caster sugar and water to create a stock syrup. Dice the kiwi, the pineapple and mango into half inch square cubes and the papaya into lengths. Add the pineapple and mango to the boiling syrup, add the papaya, and when cool add the kiwi.

Chantilly

Whip the cream with the vanilla seeds. Sweeten with the sugar.

Rum liquor

Add all ingredients and bring to the boil to a syrupy constistency.

SIMPSONS

20 Highfield Road, Edgbaston, Birmingham B15 3DX
Tel: 0121 454 3434
www.simpsonsrestaurant.co.uk

THAI EDGE

*Chef Mit
Jeensanthia*

THAI EDGE

At Thai Edge we aim to provide the very best in Thai cuisine in a specially designed contemporary Oriental setting providing a most exciting and memorable dining experience.

Thai cuisine is popular for its subtle blending of flavours, utilising herbs and roots such as lemongrass, basil, coriander, galangal, krachai, ginger, garlic and chillies.

There are four different traditional styles of Thai cooking, each prepared, cooked and presented in perfect harmony with the surroundings.

Northern cuisine – is rich and mild, making good use of coconut milk and green curry.

North-Eastern cuisine – is spicy. Dried chillies feature in the red curry, an influence of both Laos and Cambodia.

Central cuisine – for those with a mild palate, concentrates on the use of coconut, lemon and basil leaves (influenced by the Chinese).

Southern cuisine – the spiciest food of all, influenced by Malaysia and India.

Thais have no strict rules about eating and there are no set courses as in the West. All the dishes are served at the same time, allowing everyone around the table to choose from a variety of tastes and textures. Dishes are not eaten in any particular order. The dishes should be as varied as possible, mild with spicy, grilled with soupy, fish accompanying meat. The rule of thumb is the more variety the better. The absolute minimum is a soup and two main dishes – with rice of course.

All this adds Sanuk, or fun, to the meal.

Tom Kah Gai (chicken in coconut milk)

INGREDIENTS

300g chicken (cut into 1cm x 2.5cm pieces)

5-6 red birdeye chillis

400ml coconut milk

2 crushed shallot

4-5 slices galangal (a close relative of ginger)

2 kaffir lime leaves

2tbsp fish sauce

3tbsp lime juice

1 stalk lemon grass (cut into 4 pieces)

200ml chicken stock

1tsp sugar

Coriander to garnish

METHOD

Bring the stock to the boil over medium heat. Add the coconut milk, galangal, lemon grass, kaffir lime leaves, shallots and chillis, the chicken, fish sauce, sugar and lime juice. Simmer for five minutes or until the chicken is cooked. Remove the contents into a serving bowl and garnish with fresh coriander.

THAI EDGE
7 Oozells Square, Brindleyplace, Birmingham B1 2HL
Tel: 0121 643 3993

Gaeng Keow Waan Gai
(chicken green curry)

INGREDIENTS

Green curry paste

2 stalks lemon grass (cut into 13mm pieces)

1tbsp galangal

1tbsp cumin

$^1/_2$ cup fresh coriander root

8 garlic cloves

10 green Thai chilli peppers

1tsp shrimp paste

$^1/_4$tsp minced kaffir lime skin

Pinch of salt

6 fresh kaffir lime leaves

1tbsp chopped shallot

400ml coconut milk

450g chicken (cut into 1cm x 2.5cm pieces)

60ml fish sauce (nam pla)

3tbsp sugar

1 cup Thai eggplant or diced aubergines

A few sweet basil leaves to garnish

2tbsp cooking oil

METHOD

Place all the green curry paste ingredients in an electric blender and process until smooth.

Heat the oil in a large saucepan or wok, add the green curry paste and stir until it is well-mixed.

Pour half of the coconut milk into the saucepan/wok and heat until boiled. Add the chicken, fish sauce, sugar and eggplant and simmer for two to three minutes. Pour the rest of the coconut milk and simmer, stirring to combine the ingredients. Add the sweet basil leaves and then remove into a serving bowl and garnish with red chilli and sweet basil.

Serve with steamed rice.

THAI EDGE

7 Oozells Square, Brindleyplace, Birmingham B1 2HL

Tel: 0121 643 3993

Tago

INGREDIENTS

$1/2$ cup corn flour	1 cup diced water chestnuts
2 cups coconut milk	$1^1/_2$ cup sago
2tbsp sugar (for the topping)	1 cup sugar (for the base)
1tsp salt	2 cups water (for the base)

METHOD

For the base

Boil the water over a medium heat and gently add the sago. Keep stirring gently until they are cooked and opaque and slightly sticky. Add the cup of sugar and the water chestnuts and reduce heat.

For the topping

In a separate pan, add sugar and salt to the coconut milk, bring to boil. Blend corn flour with a little water until they are well-mixed but not too runny, then pour the corn flour into the coconut milk. Lower the heat and stir gently until the mixture becomes thicker.

Prepare square mould 1in square, 1in deep. Pour about $1/_2$in of the first mixture (the sago) into a mould, top with coconut milk mixture until it is full. Leave to set.

THAI EDGE
7 Oozells Square, Brindleyplace, Birmingham B1 2HL
Tel: 0121 643 3993

CONTRIBUTORS

BAR ESTILO
110 -114 Wharfside Street, The Mailbox,
Birmingham B1 1RF
Tel: 0121 643 3443
www.barestilo.co.uk

CAFÉ IKON
Ikon Gallery, 1 Oozells Square,
Brindleyplace, Birmingham B1 2HS
Tel: 0121 248 3226

CITY CAFÉ
City Inn Birmingham, 1 Brunswick Square,
Brindleyplace, Birmingham B1 2HW
Tel: 0121 633 6300
www.citycafe.co.uk

CORNERFLAG RESTAURANT
Villa Park, Birmingham B6 6HE
Tel: 0121 326 1519

DEL VILLAGGIO
245 Broad Street, Birmingham B1 2HQ
Tel: 0121 643 4224
www.del-villaggio.com

FINO CAFÉ BAR & RESTAURANT
120 -122 Wharfside Street, The Mailbox,
Birmingham B1 1RD
Tel: 0121 632 1232

JONATHANS' HOTEL AND RESTAURANT
16 Wolverhampton Road, Oldbury, West
Midlands B68 0LH
Tel: 0121 429 3757
www.jonathans-birmingham.com

THE LIVING ROOM
Unit 4, Regency Wharf 2, Broad Street,
Birmingham B1 2JZ
Tel: 0870 44 22 539
www.thelivingroom.co.uk

MACKENZIE'S BAR AND DINING ROOM
5 The Citadel, 190 Corporation Street,
Birmingham B4 6QD
Tel: 0121 236 4009
www.mackenziesbaranddiningroom.com

MIXATMECHU
47 Summerrow, Birmingham B3 1JJ
Tel: 0121 710 4222
www.summerrow.com
pippa@summerrow.com

MIYAKO TEPPANYAKI
China Town, Arcadian Centre, Ladywell Walk,
Hurst Street, Birmingham B5 4ST
Tel: 0121 622 5183

PRANA RESTAURANT & LOUNGE
121 Suffolk Street (located by The Mailbox),
Birmingham B1 1LX
Tel: 0121 616 2211
www.pranarestaurant.co.uk

RED PEPPERS
117 Wharfside Street, The Mailbox,
Birmingham B1 1RF
Tel: 0121 643 4202

SANCTUM
110 Colmore Row, Birmingham B3 3AG
Tel: 0121 236 1110
www.sanctumbirmingham.com

SIMPLY SIMPSONS
101-103 Warwick Road, Kenilworth,
Warwickshire CV8 1HL
Tel: 01926 864567
www.simpsonsrestaurant.co.uk

SIMPSONS
20 Highfield Road, Edgbaston,
Birmingham B15 3DX
Tel: 0121 454 3434
www.simpsonsrestaurant.co.uk

THAI EDGE
7 Oozells Square, Brindleyplace,
Birmingham B1 2HL
Tel: 0121 643 3993

STORE CUPBOARD

BASICS
Rice: Basmati, arborio, brown
Mustard: Dijon, wholegrain, mustard powder
Oils: Olive, canola, vegetable, sesame, walnut
Vinegars: Red, white wine, balsamic, chinese rice
Flour: Plain, self raising
Dried chillies
Bay leaves
Root ginger
Cous cous
Salt: Sea, cooking, table

Sugar: Brown, white
Tinned tomatoes
Pulses: Borlotti, cannelloni, butter Beans, chickpeas
Lentils: Brown, red
Nuts: Cashew, pistachio, walnut
Almonds: blanched, whole, flaked, slivered
Coconut milk
Cooking chocolate and cocoa powder – 70%
Sauces: Soya, fish, oyster
Anchovies

FRESH HERBS
Basil
Coriander
Rosemary
Thyme
Sage
Bay
Mint
Dill
Chervil

SPICES
Curry leaves
Turmeric powder

Cinnamon powder
Clove powder
Nutmeg powder
Chilli powder
Coriander powder
Cumin seeds
Coriander seeds
Cardamom pods
Fennel seeds
Mustard seeds
Caraway seeds
Peppercorns
Garam Masala
Star anise

EQUIPMENT

RECOMMENDED
Baking parchment For non-stick effect.
Cake spatula For easing out cakes from tins.
Casserole Preferably cast iron, 5 pint = family size.
Chinois Metal conical sieve with fine mesh.
Colander Metal, with handles.
Dariole Small cylindrical mould.
Digital scales Considered to be the most accurate.
Draining spoon Metal, longhandled.
Food processor Good quality multi-purpose, with blender.
Frying pan Eight inch and ten inch.
Grater Four-sided, easy to clean.
Kitchen timer With alarm mechanism.
Knife set Good quality cook's knives, serrated, bread, paring, carving, palette, cleaver.
Large mixing bowl Plus smaller glass bowls.

Mandolin Instrument, not musical, for finely slicing.
Measuring jugs Two varying sizes.
Pastry brush For basting.
Pastry Cutters Various shapes and sizes, preferably metal.
Pestle and morter Stone, not porcelain.
Rolling pin Wooden.
Saucepans Aluminium, stainless steel, copper-based, non-stick.
Sieves Rounded/conical.
Steamer Either freestanding or saucepan top.
Sugar thermometer Essential in confectionary and some dessert making, but also useful for fat temperature.
Tins Metal baking sheet, roasting tin, flan ring, mould, cake tins, patty tins, spring form tin, loaf tin.
Whisk Balloon/electric.
Wooden spoons Different sizes, plus wooden spatula.

Cooking terms and Methods

Bain-Marie A cooking method where the dish is cooked immersed in a half-filled tin or pan of boiling water.

Baste To coat during cooking.

Bind To blend dry and liquid ingredients.

Blanch To briefly cook in boiling water.

Blister To heat the surface of an ingredient. For example: peppers, until the skin blisters.

Blitz To rapidly blend or heat ingredients.

Brown To cook until surface starts to brown.

Caramelise To heat sugar or sugar syrup until it browns to a caramel colour.

Chinois Very fine sieve.

Compote A thick purée of fruit.

Concasse Coarsely chopped ingredients.

Confit Meat cooked in own fat and then preserved encased in fat to prevent contact with air.

Consommé A light clear soup/sauce.

Coulis A light fruit sauce.

Croquant Biscuit, from French for crunchy or crisp.

Croustillant A dish either presented on, or enclosed in, a shell of pastry.

Debearded A term applying to preparation of shellfish, where little hairs have been removed.

Deskirted Another shellfish term referring to trimming and cleaning of scallops.

Deglaze To heat a liquid, usually stock or wine, with pan juices as basis for gravy.

Demiglace Rich, concentrated brown stock, can be bought ready-made.

Dice Finely chop.

Flambé To flame a mixture containing alcohol.

Flash-fry To quickly fry.

Fold To gently combine ingredients with a metal spoon or knife.

Glaze To coat food with egg, milk or syrup before or after cooking.

Infuse To immerse strong flavoured ingredients in hot liquid, which is then left to stand for a while eg vanilla pods in milk.

Jus A clear stock or pure fruit juice.

Knead A technique applied in perfecting dough, done by hand on a floured board.

Macerate To steep in alcohol or syrup, in order to flavour or soften.

Marinade A mixture in which meat, fish or other ingredients are soaked before cooking.

Napping To coat an item with sauce.

Noisette Small piece of meat, usually the eye of a chop.

Parboil To partly boil, from five to 15 minutes.

Poach To cook food at just below boiling point for a protracted time.

Prove The second stage in bread making, where dough is allowed to rise after shaping.

Quenelle To roll or shape into a ball.

Refresh Plunging just boiled or blanched vegetables into cold water, to preserve fresh colour.

Rillette A coarse paté.

Roux The butter and flour base to sauces – flour is added to melted butter and cooked into a paste for a minute before adding liquid.

Reduce To boil rapidly to reduce liquid content and concentrate flavour.

Sauté To lightly fry.

Sear To rapidly pan-cook meat at a high temperature.

Strain To pass liquid through a sieve to free it of lumps.

Sweat To seal in a covered pan.

Terrine A layered and set loaf-shaped starter, often incorporating meat.

Turn To shape with a knife or peeler, whilst rotating, into a regular, round shape.

Whipping To beat quickly with a spoon or whisk to incorporate air.

GLOSSARY

Allspice berry From the West Indian allspice tree. When ground, it has the aroma and taste of a combination of cinnamon, cloves, nutmeg and pepper.

Borlotti bean A large, plump bean, pinkish brown in colour with reddish brown streaks, available dried or tinned. Widely used in Italian cooking.

Cardamon The seeds are contained in small pods, which you crush to remove the seeds. Strong aroma and a warm, spicy-sweet flavour.

Cane syrup Golden syrup.

Capers Pickled flower buds of a shrub native to the Mediterranean and parts of Asia. Usually bought in jars.

Chervil An aromatic herb, like tarragon, with lacy leaves.

Chilli oil Bought ready-bottled from supermarkets.

Chinese wine Available from Chinese supermarkets. Use dry sherry as substitute.

Chorizo A Spanish sausage, spicy in flavour and made of ground pork.

Celeriac Root vegetable cooked like potato, with distinctive celery taste.

Cinnamon sticks Cinnamon bark in stick form, available from good supermarkets.

Cous cous A fine cereal made from semolina.

Five spice powder Chinese spice containing cinnamon, cloves, fennel, star anise and Sichuan peppers.

Harrisa North African hot paste.

Kirsch A liqueur distilled from crushed cherries and their stones.

Lardons Small, chunky strips – usually of bacon or pork.

Lemon grass Stalk used in Chinese and Thai cookery. Discard outer husk and crush inner stem for lemon flavour.

Mache A green salad leaf native to Europe with dark green leaves and tangy flavour. Also called field salad, field lettuce and lamb's lettuce.

Maris Piper Versatile, good quality potato.

Mange tout Whole pea pods, eaten young and blanched.

Manzanilla A very dry, pale sherry from Spain.

Marsala Fortified wine produced in Marsala, Sicily.

Mascarpone Italian soft cheese, often used in desserts.

Pak choy Chinese cabbage with a mild mustard taste.

Port wine sauce A traditional, rich sauce that can be bought ready-prepared.

Root ginger Thick root of a tropical plant, can be frozen.

Saffron Vibrant natural colorant, extracted from crocuses.

Salmon keta A small salmon, native to the Pacific Coast of America.

Saltpeter Potassium nitrate, used in preservation of meat. Available from chemists or online.

Savoyarde biscuits Traditional dessert biscuits, readily available.

Scallops Shellfish available in a range of sizes, with delicate taste.

Soy sauce Made from fermented soy beans. Use dark for extra colour, light for flavour and salty taste.

Star anise Star-shaped seed pods with distinctive taste, available from Chinese supermarkets.

Tuile A French biscuit, moulded into curved shape while still hot.

Turmeric Spice used in Indian cooking, mainly for its bright yellow colour.

Vanilla pod Fragrant dried pods of the vanilla orchid.

CONVERSION TABLES

TEMPERATURE

GAS	ELECTRIC DEGREES F	ELECTRIC DEGREES C
1	275	140 very cool
2	300	150 cool
3	325	170 warm
4	350	180 moderate
5	375	190 fairly hot
6	400	200 hot
7	425	220 very hot
8	450	230 very hot
9	475	240 very hot

WEIGHTS

1oz	25g
2	50g
3	75g
4	110g
5	150g
6	175g
7	200g
8	225g
9	250g
10	275g
12	350g
1lb	450g
1.5lb	700g
2lb	900g
3lb	1.3kg

LIQUIDS

2fl oz	60ml
3	90ml
5	150ml
10	300ml
15	450ml
1 pint	600ml
1.25	750ml
1.75	1 litre
2	1.2
2.5	1.5

INDEX OF RECIPES BY COURSE

DESSERTS

NOTES

NOTES